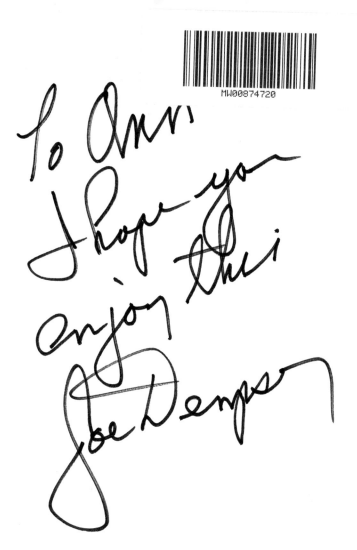

To Anri
I hope you
enjoy this

Joe Dempsey

1

The Harder
The Conflict

A Historical Novel of the
American Revolution for
Young Adults

Joseph H. Dempsey

The Harder the Conflict

A Historical Novel of the American Revolution for Young Adults

Joseph H. Dempsey

Copyright © 2008 Joseph H. Dempsey

ISBN 143826416X

EAN-13 9781438264165

Cover Design by Kristin Taylor Larcom

"These are the times that try men's souls. The summer soldier and the sunshine patriot will, in this crisis, shrink from the service of their country, but he that stands it now, deserves the love and thanks of man and woman. Tyranny, like hell, is not easily conquered; yet we have this consolation with us, that <u>The Harder the Conflict</u>, the more glorious the triumph. What we obtain too cheap, we esteem too lightly; 'tis dearness only that gives everything its value. Heaven knows how to put a proper price upon its goods, and it would be strange indeed, if so celestial an article as freedom should not be highly rated."

Thomas Paine <u>The American Crisis</u>

December 23, 1776

Chapter One
The Powder Mill
Morristown, NJ

Beavers like slow-moving water. The Whippanong River, as it flows through Morristown, is not more than forty feet wide; not more than four feet deep. It is an ideal place for those creatures with such beautiful fur. The river has ample growth along its banks to provide the sticks and branches for the beaver dams.

This early July day twelve-year old Jimmy Stiles was looking for those dams with hopes he might see one of the shy beavers. The boy was fascinated with these animals that swim so well and build such intricate, underwater homes.

The river twisted and turned as it meandered through the woods. Jimmy hadn't been in this section of the river since last fall but he knew from memory every one of those twists and turns. He was approaching the area where, at one of the bends, an island had formed. The main part of the river flowed to the left; a smaller stream to the right, creating the island as the two parts rejoined further down. The undergrowth here was thick and Jimmy had to crawl along the bank if he were to keep his eye on the stream. He was about a mile from the Morristown Green, the center of town, and had seen several beaver dams but, as yet, no beaver. Suddenly he heard voices ahead.

"That's strange," he thought, "who would be out here?" Jimmy peered ahead through the underbrush but could see nothing. He crawled forward under some briar bushes until he could see three men about a hundred feet downstream unloading a wagon and taking cases of something into a building. Last fall, when he was at this part of the river, there was no building there.

About twenty feet away, to the right, was a large buttonwood tree. Jimmy wriggled over to it and very carefully stood up. Using the tree trunk to keep out of sight, he peeked around it. The building, about thirty feet long and twenty feet wide, was on the island. A water wheel, attached to the building, was in the stream. It looked like one of the grist mills where his father took wheat to be ground into flour. The men were now inside, but then two came out. Jimmy could see them plainly now and recognized both. The big man was Mr. Hathaway. The other was Mr. Ford.

"Boy! What are you doing there?"

The stern voice startled him. He turned quickly, tripped over a fallen branch and fell flat on his face. He looked up to see a man, twenty or thirty feet away, with a musket pointed right at him.

"Get up, boy and get over here." the man ordered. Jimmy stumbled toward him, so frightened he was unable to speak.

"What are you doing here?" the man demanded.

Getting his voice back Jimmy stammered "I--I was looking for beaver, sir. I didn't mean any harm."

"Walk over there to that wagon." the man gestured.

Regaining his usual grit, Jimmy said, "Don't point that gun at me, sir. I told you I meant no harm." The man lowered the musket but gave him a shove and they both walked toward the wagon.

As they approached, Mr. Hathaway turned toward them and recognized Jimmy. "Jimmy Stiles, what are you doing here?"

"I was looking for beaver, Mr. Hathaway. I didn't mean any trouble."

"Put the musket away, Elijah. The boy is no danger." said Benoni Hathaway. "Jimmy, I have a surprise for you. Captain Joseph, come here and see who came to visit us."

The third man came to the door of the building and looked out. He was much older than the others. Jimmy shouted out, "Grandpa! What are you doing here? What's going on?"

'Hello, Jimmy. I'll bet I know what you're doing here." Turning to Benoni Hathaway he said, "Ben, Jimmy loves to study beavers. He's been fascinated with them since he first saw one. I should have known he would find this place."

Jacob Ford said to Jimmy's grandfather, "Captain Joseph, maybe you'd better explain all this to him. Now that he's seen the powder mill he has to be sworn to secrecy."

'You're right, Jake. We're done here for today. I'll explain everything on our trip back to town. Climb in the wagon everyone. Elijah, you take the reins. Ben, you sit up with him. I have some explaining to do."

Captain Joseph Stiles climbed in the back of the wagon and motioned for his grandson to sit beside him. Benoni Hathaway and Elijah

Freeman climbed in the front. Jacob Ford took a place beside Jimmy.

Joseph Stiles was seventy years old and had lived in Morristown since he was fourteen. During the French and Indian War Joseph became a member of the Morris Militia where he served as a captain. Ever since, everybody in Morristown called him Captain Joseph.

Jimmy's home was in New Vernon, about four miles from Morristown. His father, also named Joseph, had a farm there. For the past few months Jimmy had a job as an errand boy at Arnold's Tavern on the edge of The Green in the center of Morristown. Most of the time he walked home after work but sometimes he stayed at his grandparents' home in Morristown. Jimmy was a likeable youngster and knew almost everybody in town. He was smart, too, for a twelve year-old. While working at Arnold's he would often listen to the men talk about events in the country. He knew there was trouble with the British. He knew about the fighting at Lexington and Concord a year before. So, when Grandpa Stiles began to explain the purpose of the mill Jimmy clearly understood what he was talking about.

The wagon was proceeding on a narrow path through the dense woods that hid the location of the mill from prying eyes. The path led away from the river to the Whippany Road. As the wagon lurched along, Grandpa began his explanation.

"Jimmy," he said, "the mill you just saw is a gunpowder mill. We are going to make gunpowder there. With the war going on in Massachusetts it won't be long before it comes here and there is a terrible shortage of gunpowder. We've heard that the army has only enough gunpowder for each soldier to fire his musket nine times. The British have prohibited the making of gunpowder in the colonies and, since 1774, have stopped any shipment of gunpowder to the colonies. The punishment for making gunpowder is hanging. If the British find out we're making gunpowder here, you can be sure they will come looking, just as they did at Lexington and Concord. That's why what you saw today must be kept secret. You must tell no one what you saw."

"Do you know how to make gunpowder, Grandpa? What do you use to make it?" asked Jimmy.

"Mr. Ford knows how. He's our expert. He'll answer your question." replied Grandpa.

"Jimmy," Jacob Ford explained, "to make gunpowder you need three ingredients: charcoal, sulfur and saltpeter. You mix it together–three parts saltpeter, one part sulfur and about one part charcoal. You can make a small amount by hand but to make a lot, like what the army needs, you have to have a mill like we built back by the river. The saltpeter, sulfur and charcoal must be ground into a fine powder. We were carrying the ingredients into the mill when you found us. Jimmy, I know you're only twelve years old but I have to swear you to secrecy. You must keep this secret about the mill even if it means death. I think the best way to do that is to make you a member of the militia. If any of your friends find out about the mill, you must tell me or your Grandpa at once. Do you understand?"

"Yes sir, Mr. Ford. I understand. Am I really a soldier now?" asked Jimmy.

"That's Colonel Ford, Jimmy, of the Morris Militia." said Grandpa. "Yes, you are a soldier but only if you agree to be one."

"I do." answered Jimmy, "And I swear to keep this secret."

Colonel Ford continued. "Jimmy, five days ago the British put a large force of soldiers on Staten Island, just across Arthur Kill from Elizabethtown. That means British soldiers are not much more than a day's march from Morristown. I also received news today from Philadelphia that three days ago, on July Fourth, the members of the Continental Congress declared independence from Britain. The British are not going to stand by and allow us to declare independence. For sure, if the British find out about this powder mill, Morristown will be their target. As I said before, Morristown will be just like Lexington and Concord. We all have to be alert and especially careful that the wrong people don't find out about the powder mill."

Elijah Freeman stopped the wagon. They were at the end of the path and about to enter Whippany Road, but were still hidden by the woods. Elijah and Benoni Hathaway looked carefully both ways. They didn't want anyone to see them emerging from the woods. That might give away the location of the mill. When they were sure it was safe they moved out onto Whippany Road. Just down the road was Jacob Ford's house. When they reached it, he got off, but before leaving said, "Remember, Jimmy. This is a secret. You are a member of the militia and must guard that secret with your life. When you work in the tavern and hear any talk about the mill you must report it immediately. Keep your eyes and ears open. I'll have more work for you soon. Meanwhile, even though you're a member of the militia I want you to keep that to yourself, too. A twelve-year old member is quite unusual and might get people wondering why. Just remember, you are more help to me using your eyes and ears."

The wagon moved on toward the Morristown Green where Benoni Hathaway got off. Elijah proceeded across the Green to Arnold's Tavern where Jimmy and Captain Joseph got off. Elijah told Captain Joseph he was going on to James Young's farm in Mendham to pick up a load of sulfur and would be back before sundown. Captain Joseph told him to put the wagon with the sulfur in the shed behind the tavern. They would take it to the mill tomorrow.

"Jimmy, are you coming home with me or going to your Pa's?" Grandpa asked.

"I have a few chores to do for Mr. Arnold. Then I'm walking home. Pa needs me for some jobs on the farm tomorrow. Say hello to Grandma for me."

Jimmy walked into the tavern and began to sweep the big room. When finished he said good-bye to Mr. Arnold, told him he would be back the day after tomorrow, and left. The mid-July afternoon sun beat down on Jimmy as he trudged homeward on the Vealtown Road.

Chapter Two

The Lookouts

Summer and Fall 1776

The people of Morristown were very nervous during the summer of 1776. Earlier in the year the British left Boston and moved to Halifax, Nova Scotia. General George Washington quickly moved into Boston but believed the British would sooner or later leave Halifax to try to capture New York. He decided to move his army to New York City. It was the right move. On July 2 the British occupied Staten Island at the entrance into New York harbor. The enemy was very close to Morristown—only thirty-five miles away, but separated and protected by the Watchung Mountains.

Jimmy Stiles noticed the nervousness among the people of Morristown. By August the militia had begun their drills on the Green across the street from Arnold's Tavern. In the tavern's big room, men, sitting at the tables, talked about how close the British were and wondered if they would come to Morristown and burn homes as they had already done in Elizabethtown.

Jimmy followed Colonel Ford's order. He watched and listened to what was going on. As he waited on customers he had the opportunity to hear much of their conversations. The customers hardly noticed his presence and talked freely as if he were not there. Jimmy learned many things from those conversations. At the end of August he learned about the British attack on General Washington's soldiers on Long Island. He learned that the Americans barely escaped capture as they crossed the East River from Brooklyn into Manhattan. Several weeks later he learned the British had seized all of Manhattan and pushed the Americans northward. At the end of October he heard about the battle and the defeat at White Plains. The news was not good. He could see that the people at the tavern were worried.

In early November, while waiting on a group of men he had never seen before, he heard one of them use the words "gunpowder mill." But he heard nothing more. Nevertheless, he did what Colonel Ford told him to do and immediately went to his grandfather and told him what happened.

Shortly after, forty miles away in New York City, a British army lieutenant, John Montresor, was busy drawing a map of Morristown. He marked a spot on the map to show the location of a powder mill. A British spy living in the Morristown area had supplied that information. Lieutenant Montresor's map was accurate and was to guide a raiding party to destroy the mill. What Lieutenant Montresor didn't know was that an American spy knew what the lieutenant was doing and told the American authorities. Within a short time Colonel Ford was alerted and began to make ready for a possible visit from British soldiers.

Colonel Ford assembled the Morris Militia on the Green to prepare them for action at a moment's notice. Later, the Colonel came to the tavern to find Jimmy. Out of sight of others Colonel Ford asked Jimmy to take a walk with him. Behind the tavern, about a quarter mile to the south, was a steep hill called Kinney's Hill. It not only overlooked Morristown, but also the eastern approach to the town for a distance of ten to fifteen miles. From that spot the approach of an enemy force could be detected. Colonel Ford brought a spy glass with him and, as they walked up the hill, showed Jimmy how to use it. When they reached the top Colonel Ford pointed out the Watchung Mountains off to the east. "Those mountains run north to south, Jimmy. They are an obstacle to the British. Between the mountains and Morristown there is about ten miles of flat land, some of it swamp and difficult to travel through."

Using the spy glass, Colonel Ford showed Jimmy a small gap in the mountains and explained, "If British soldiers come to Morristown, Jimmy, they will come through that gap. It's called Hobart Gap. We have lookouts there who will signal us that the British are coming. Their view of Elizabethtown is as clear as our view of the gap. They have built a tower at the gap and will set it afire when they spot the British. What I want you to do is gather some of your friends and organize them as lookouts. When one of you sees that fire, you are to run as fast as you can to the Green and sound the alarm. Do you think you can do this, Jimmy?"

"I think so, Colonel Ford. I know my best friend, Sam Hathaway, will help and there's also Caleb Fairchild and Benjamin Trowbridge. Phebe Aber is a good friend. Can girls be lookouts, too?"

"Their eyes are just as good as boy's, if not better. Certainly, they can." replied the Colonel. "You're going to need more than a handful of helpers, though. You and your friends can watch during daylight. I'm going to get some of the older men from the militia to stand watch at night. I'll bet your Grandpa, Captain Joseph, will help. I really need the younger men to send out to meet the British if they come."

The next day Jimmy, Sam Hathaway, Caleb Fairchild, Benjamin Trowbridge and Phebe Aber got busy. They talked with their friends and got thirteen to volunteer to help. The eighteen of them gathered tools and boards went to the top of the hill and built a lookout platform high up in one of the tall oak trees. From there they could plainly see Hobart Gap. Jimmy showed them how to use the spy glass and explained what they were looking for. They decided to make teams of two to stand two hour watches from seven in the morning until five at night. At seven the next morning Jimmy and Sam took the first watch and at nine they were relieved by Phebe and her friend, Sarah Mathias. The other teams followed as their turns came up. At night the older members of the militia kept watch. Grandpa Stiles was their leader.

It was now late November. The trees had lost their leaves and the lookouts had to dress warmly when they went to the hill. Some snow had fallen but not enough to cover the ground. One night, when Grandpa Stiles returned from his watch, he was soaked to the skin. A sudden rain had come. Of course, Grandpa stayed until he was relieved. The next day he came down with a bad cold but after several days he seemed to get better. Though he had a cough he was determined to go back to his every day activities.

December 1 was a Sunday. Grandpa was a deacon at the Morristown Presbyterian Church and insisted he was going to church even though he still had a bad cough. He and Grandma were there every Sunday and Grandpa was not going to let a cough stop him. Like most of the members, Grandma and Grandpa walked to church. Jimmy had spent the night with them and, though he belonged to the Basking Ridge Church, this Sunday he went to church with his grandparents.

The Presbyterian Church was located next to the Green. It was not large but was big enough for all the members. There was a wide center aisle. The women sat to the left, the men to the right. The eldest members sat in the front rows so they could hear. There were two balconies, one on each side, with a stairway to each balcony. The unmarried men and boys sat in the left balcony; the unmarried women and girls in the right. In each balcony was a man called a "beadle" whose responsibility was to keep order among the young people. If any fell asleep during services the beadle woke them. He had a long thin rod with a metal tip and the dozer felt the metal tip with enough force to improve his attention. The misbehaving youth felt the metal tip with much greater force. Walking in front of the adult section was the "liner." Many people in the congregation could not read so the liner's responsibility was to read from the hymnal a line and then the congregation would sing that line of the hymn.

Grandpa Stiles was a deacon and therefore sat on the aisle. Because he was seventy he sat near the front in the third row. From the balcony Jimmy could look down on Grandpa. The congregation was singing the first hymn of the services when there was a crash and Jimmy saw Grandpa had collapsed into the aisle. The liner was the first to get to Grandpa. Grandma rushed from the other side. Jimmy ran to the stairs to get to his Grandfather. Grandpa was unconscious and felt very hot. Reverend Johnes, an old man himself, ordered the men to lift Grandpa up on to one of the pews. They could not wake him and after several minutes someone brought a wagon to the church door. They put Grandpa in the back on some straw. Grandma, Jimmy and several other men got in and the driver took them to Grandpa's house. The men carried Grandpa in and laid him on his bed. He never woke up. With Grandma, Jimmy and Reverend Johnes at his side, Grandpa died shortly after midnight.

At Grandpa's funeral Reverend Johnes said Captain Joseph was a hero. Though he didn't carry a musket and bayonet he was doing his duty as a lookout atop Kinney's Hill and stayed at his post through a cold, driving rain. He used Grandpa as an example of the kind of perseverance the people would have to show in the coming days ahead. After the service Grandpa was buried in the cemetery behind the church.

The next day, Jimmy and Sam were back on the hill looking for the signal from Hobart Gap. In town a group of soldiers appeared. Rumors had spread that they were part of General Washington's army retreating from the British and that the army would be coming soon to Morristown.

Colonel Ford knew better. He knew that General Washington was headed for Pennsylvania. The general had requested militia from all over New Jersey to cover his retreat until the army reached the Delaware River. Colonel Ford ordered several hundred Morris militiamen to Chatham, about two miles from Hobart Gap and ten miles from Morristown, to be close to

Washington's retreating army. The militia could reach Hobart Gap quickly if needed. Colonel Ford kept a larger force in reserve at Morristown and placed Colonel John Symmes in charge of the militiamen in Chatham. A signal system was created using a series of cannon blasts. Colonel Symmes was told that if he heard three successive cannon firings he was to march immediately to Hobart Gap where he would get further information.

That evening Jimmy walked home to New Vernon. After his chores and supper he went to bed but was wakened very early in the morning when he heard a group of horsemen outside the house. He ran to the door and looked out. One of the horsemen saw him and hollered out, "Which way to Basking Ridge?"

Jimmy didn't respond but pointed to the east--not the way to Basking Ridge. Jimmy realized the men were British soldiers and he wasn't going to give them any help. Another voice said, "He's just a boy. He can't help us. Let's keep moving on." The soldiers moved on and Jimmy went back into the house.

"What did they want?" asked Jimmy's father.

"They wanted to know how to get to Basking Ridge so I pointed towards the east." answered Jimmy.

"Good boy, Jimmy. I wonder what they're after? That's the first group of British soldiers I've seen."

Jimmy went back to bed wondering if they were searching for the gunpowder mill. The next morning he was walking back to work and was picked up by two men in a wagon. He got in the back and listened as they talked. They were discussing an incident that happened early that morning. A British patrol on horseback had raided White's Tavern and captured General Charles Lee. The patrol escaped with the General before anyone could rescue him.

"That must have been the soldiers I saw last night," he thought. "I guess they weren't after the powder mill, but if they can reach Basking Ridge without being seen we had better be more alert."

When he reached the tavern, the raid was the talk of everyone. The appearance of the British soldiers and the news of the raid made everyone jittery.

Jimmy learned that the new soldiers in town had come from Fort Ticonderoga on orders from General Washington and that more were coming. General Washington wanted troops to protect his flank and cover his rear as he retreated across New Jersey toward Pennsylvania. Jimmy knew that something unusual was happening. He had to tell all the lookouts to be especially watchful.

It didn't take long. It was a mid-December afternoon. Jimmy and Sam had just completed their watch and had been relieved by Phebe and Sarah. As the two boys were walking down the hill they heard Phebe shout, "A fire! A fire! It's the signal."

The boys ran back to the top. They could plainly see the fire at Hobart Gap. "Let's go!" shouted Jimmy and the four started running down the hill. When they got to Arnold's Tavern, Jimmy shouted the alarm.

Colonel Ford had trained the militia members well. Immediately, several men ran for the cannon on the Green and within minutes had fired the three shots. Three more men ran for their horses and were off to Chatham, ten miles away, to report to Colonel Symmes just in case the cannon shots were not heard. The alarm, calling the militia to the Green, had been given and by nightfall several hundred men, under the leadership of Colonel Ford, were marching to Hobart Gap. Before they left the Green, Jimmy came to Colonel Ford and asked, "Colonel, let me come with you. I could be your messenger. You know I'm reliable."

At first the Colonel was about to say "no." He paused for a moment, then said, "Jimmy, go to your Grandma's house, get her horse, and tell your Grandma I need you with me as a messenger. Tell her I need someone who can get back to Morristown in case we need more help. Then catch up with the militia and join us. You and your friends earned my trust today."

Jimmy ran down Bridge Street to Grandma's. He gave her Colonel Ford's message, ran to the barn to saddle up Prince and was off to catch up with the militia.

The next morning people of Morristown gathered on the Green to await news. A rider from Hobart Gap had arrived during the night with news that a British force of eight hundred men under the command of General Alexander Leslie had crossed Arthur Kill from Staten Island and were marching on Morristown. That news increased the fear and anxiety among the townspeople. They had fathers, sons, and brothers who were about to fight the British and they were worried.

December 17, 1776 was a very long day in Morristown. Shortly after nine in the evening a horseman galloped into town with news that the British had been stopped at Springfield with very light militia casualties. The rider was Jimmy Stiles. He reported that the militia met the British in late afternoon near the Springfield Church. The British didn't expect the militia in such force. After a short skirmish and with darkness fast approaching the British quickly turned around and marched back to Staten Island.

The people had gathered on the Green and, cheered by the news, surrounded Jimmy to get more details.

"There isn't much to tell," explained Jimmy. "They came at us in ranks with their bayonets fixed. I guess they thought that would scare us but the men held their ground. I think the Redcoats looked to their right and left and saw that we had more men than they did with even more coming. Before a full-scale battle broke out the British realized the militia wasn't going to panic and run, so they turned around and left. I hope the next time they come it will be as easy."

After the people on the Green drifted away, Phebe Aber came to Jimmy and took his hand. "Jimmy, I'm so proud of you," and then she ran away across the Green.

The people of Morristown were about to be tested again. The same day as the action at Springfield General Alexander McDougal arrived in town to take leadership of more troops coming from Fort Ticonderoga. Those troops were to be added to General Washington's army but their arrival in Morristown unintentionally brought a deadly gift for the townspeople.

Chapter Three

The Pox

Winter and Spring 1776-1777

In mid-December General William Howe, who had been pursuing the Americans across New Jersey, stopped the chase when the Americans crossed into Pennsylvania. He sent his main force back to New York for the winter and left a group of soldiers at Trenton and Princeton. On Christmas Day the Americans re-crossed the Delaware River and attacked the British troops at Trenton. Several days later they attacked the British again, this time at Princeton. With victories at both places General Washington moved his army northward to Morristown to settle in for the winter.

During the morning of January 6, 1777 Jimmy was working in the big room at the tavern when he heard a commotion outside. He went to the door to see what was happening. People were running across the Green and Jimmy could hear drums beating in the distance. He went outside and soon saw a tall man on horseback followed by many soldiers on foot. He looked closely and realized it was General Washington and the army.

There were about four hundred troops from

Fort Ticonderoga already in Morristown. That's a lot of additional people for a small town. Now, with General Washington's arrival there would be more soldiers–many more, perhaps as many as four thousand more. The townspeople and those other people, who lived within a radius of ten miles, took as many soldiers into their homes as they could. The rest were encamped a few miles southeast of Morristown in Loantica Valley. General Washington and much of his staff made their headquarters on the second floor of Arnold's Tavern.

As soon as he was sure it was General Washington, Jimmy rushed back into the tavern to tell Mr. Arnold. Jimmy had been busy that morning and the day before cleaning up the rooms on the second floor. The General's office would be there. He would sleep in another room and his staff would stay in other sections of the tavern. Mr. Arnold gave Jimmy the job of cleaning the General's rooms and of making sure there was always a supply of firewood available for the General and his staff. So far, this was an exceptionally cold winter with lots of snow. Keeping firewood available was to be no easy task.

The day after General Washington arrived Jimmy was busy carrying firewood to the second floor of the tavern. There was a large wood pile behind the tavern and Jimmy had already brought up five loads. He was tired and his legs were beginning to be a little unsteady. He was on his sixth trip to the second floor and was struggling. He knew someone was behind him on the stairs and when he got to the top he heard a voice say,

"Young man, let me have some of those logs. You look worn out."

Jimmy turned and saw General Washington. The General began to take some of the logs from Jimmy's arms and stacked them by the fireplace.

"Thank you, sir" said Jimmy. "I was getting a little tired."

"This is Jimmy Stiles, General." a man behind the General said. "He is quite a soldier."

It was Benoni Hathaway speaking. "Jimmy, Colonel Ford is quite sick and is in bed at his home. He hasn't been well since the action at Springfield. He asked me to take his place as the leader of the militia until he is better." Benoni Hathaway continued, "General, when we were at Springfield last month, Colonel Ford brought

Jimmy along to serve as a messenger. As the British approached, the Colonel sent Jimmy forward with a message for me. He was there at the front at a very critical and dangerous time. There was no chance to send Jimmy to the rear before the British arrived. He stayed in the front with me. As the enemy approached we could see the sun reflecting on their bayonets. The men began to get nervous. The sight of the bayonets made many of the men very skittish. When they saw the green uniforms and the pointed hats they became even more frightened. That uniform told them they were facing the dreaded Hessians who were fighting on the side of the Redcoats. Some of our men looked as if they were about ready to turn and run. Jimmy was standing in the front row, unarmed. I hollered to the men to look at Jimmy Stiles. He's only twelve and he's not running. That steadied the men; they held. Finally, the British turned back. This boy is a brave soldier, General."

"Colonel Hathaway, do you think if I asked Mr. Arnold, he would assign this young man as my personal aide as long as I stay here at the tavern?" asked General Washington.

"General, last fall Jimmy was looking for beaver along the Whippanong River and came across the gunpowder mill. Colonel Ford swore him to secrecy and took him into the Morris County militia as a special member to insure that secrecy. He also gave Jimmy the job of organizing a group of young people as lookouts for the Hobart Gap signal. It was that group, in fact, two girls, Phebe Aber and Sarah Mathias, who sounded the alarm last December. As a member of the militia, Jimmy is already under your command. You may be sure he will do exactly what you ask of him. I know Jacob Arnold will not mind."

Jimmy couldn't believe what he was hearing. Jimmy Stiles, an aide to General Washington – wouldn't Grandpa have been proud of him? He couldn't wait to tell Grandma what happened.

Several days passed and Jimmy worked very hard to please General Washington. On January 11 news reached the tavern that Colonel Ford had died of lung fever, just as Grandpa did. The whole town was saddened. That very same day Martha Ball died. It wasn't lung fever that killed her, but smallpox. Mrs. Ball, a widow, had opened her home in December to a number of soldiers who came from Fort Ticonderoga. It was said that the British had somehow sent blankets from pox victims into the fort to spread the disease among the American soldiers. It was those soldiers who brought the disease to Morristown.

Within a few days of Mrs. Ball's death, a smallpox epidemic was raging in Morristown–especially among the several thousand soldiers who were here. The Presbyterian Church was used as a hospital but it wasn't large enough. Other buildings and homes had to be used as shelters for the sick.

General Washington asked Jimmy if he had ever had smallpox. Jimmy hadn't. The General went on, "When I was young, Jimmy, I went on a trip with my brother, Lawrence, to Barbados in the West Indies. Lawrence was sick with consumption and thought living in the islands would help him. I went along because Lawrence, who was fourteen years older, was like my father. My real father died when I was eleven. One evening Lawrence and I went to dinner at a friend's home. We didn't know it but some members of the family had smallpox. Seventeen days later I had smallpox."

"What was it like, General? How did you survive?" asked Jimmy.

"Jimmy. I was just nineteen years old then. That was twenty-five years ago. All I remember was feeling terrible–a headache, backache, fever, vomiting–then the fever came and I don't remember after that. Why did I survive? Perhaps because I was in very good health before the disease struck. Maybe I was just lucky. I do know that once you have had the pox you won't get it again."

"My mother, father and Grandma Stiles had the pox some years ago," offered Jimmy.

"Well Jimmy," responded the General, "that means they are safe. They won't get the pox. But you're not safe, so I don't want you to go anywhere near anyone who has the pox. I know that will be difficult working here at the tavern, but if you are careful you might be able to avoid it."

"I will, General. I will." answered Jimmy.

Meanwhile, the soldiers suffered terribly both from the cold winter and the pox. The sick filled the Presbyterian Church. They were laid out on the pews, in the aisle, and in the balconies on both sides of the church. In the morning those who died during the night were taken out behind the church and buried. During this time Jimmy

31

stayed at his Grandma's home for fear he might bring the disease to his home in New Vernon. His three older brothers had never had the pox.

Soon after General Washington's arrival in Morristown, Sam Hathaway was hired by Mr. Arnold to help Jimmy at the tavern. The two good friends had fun working together doing their chores. Together they kept the General's quarters clean and the fireplaces well supplied with firewood. Two days after Sam was hired he told Jimmy that his Uncle Gerhsom, had come down with the pox. Sam said that the night before he was at Uncle Gerhsom's home helping him cut firewood. On January 24th Sam didn't come to work. His uncle had died and they buried him the same day behind the church. Jimmy, remembering what General Washington had told him, worried about his friend. The next day Sam was back to work.

Several weeks later, while carrying firewood to the second floor, Sam had to stop. "Jimmy, I can't go any more. My head is aching and I'm so tired I can't move my legs."

"Why don't you go home, Sam? You look terrible." Jimmy suggested. It didn't dawn on Jimmy that Sam might be showing the first signs of the pox.

The next day Sam didn't show up for work. He lived on the opposite side of the Green and Jimmy walked the half mile to Sam's home. He knocked on the door and Sam's mother answered. "Jimmy," she said, "Sam's got the pox. His father and little John and Benoni do, too. You can't come in. I don't mean to be rude, Jimmy, but I don't want you here until Sam is well. Now get back to the tavern."

"I'm sorry, Mrs. Hathaway. Please tell Sam I was here. I hope they all get well soon. I'll be saying my prayers for them."

"Thank you, Jimmy. Now get back to work."

Sadly, Jimmy walked back to the tavern. He thought to himself, "Sam's healthy, just like the General was when he got the pox. He'll be all right."

But Sam wasn't all right. He got worse as each day passed and on February 17th, Sam died. Three days later, Sam's father Eleazar, and his brothers, John and Benoni died. Benoni was only a year old. John was five.

That same day Jimmy learned that Caleb Fairchild, Sarah Mathias and Phebe Aber had the pox. It seemed like all his friends were going to die. When he went home that night his Grandma tried to comfort him, but Jimmy was heartbroken.

The next morning when Jimmy went to work he told General Washington he was trying to avoid people with the pox but it seemed that all his friends had it. That afternoon Jimmy began to feel sick. He had a headache and realized he, too, was getting the pox. He went home and his Grandma put him to bed immediately. She then sent for Jimmy's mother and father.

In New Vernon Joseph Stiles hitched up the wagon and with his wife, Phebe, rode immediately to Morristown. They arrived at Grandma Stiles' home after the sun had gone down. Phebe Stiles told her husband not to come in. She told him to return home to look after the other boys, George, John and Joseph. "Joseph, I'm afraid you might touch something and bring home the pox to the children. I'll stay here and take care of Jimmy. I know how much you want to see him but this is for the best." Joseph knew his wife was right. He kissed her, climbed back into the wagon and turned for home.

Jimmy's mother found him asleep. She felt his head. He didn't seem to have a fever. She pulled up a chair next to the bed and settled down ready to spend the night there. Grandma Stiles placed a blanket over Phebe. "Thank you, Grandma Comfort. I think we both had better get some rest; we're going to have troubles ahead."

Very early the next morning Phebe awoke and looked at Jimmy lying in the bed next to her chair. He was still sleeping and breathing normally. She noticed red blotches on his arms and face and felt his forehead. He seemed warmer than normal but certainly not feverish.

Grandma Comfort came over to the bed. "Phebe, I think we had better get him to drink as much water as we can. There is nothing more to do except wait and hope for the best. The last time I saw smallpox was more than twenty years ago. I had recovered from it and was caring for other people who had it. There is no special treatment except to make sure they drink a lot of water and to keep them warm and still. A side effect of the pox is lung fever and in a weakened condition there is nothing that can kill you faster than that. Captain Joseph died from that."

Jimmy slept all day and toward evening his fever increased. His mother stayed right at his side holding his hand. About midnight the fever must have increased because Jimmy began to toss and turn and speak out in his sleep. He broke into a sweat and his mother kept wiping his forehead. The next morning the fever went down.

"This is the dangerous time, Phebe," explained Comfort. "Just when you think it's over, the fever comes back. The sores will appear soon. That is when the pox is most catching."

Jimmy's mother got up from the chair, walked to the door, put her cloak over her shoulders and stepped outside to get some fresh air. It was very cold and Phebe shut the door behind her. Some neighbors, passing by, asked how Jimmy was doing. Fearing to get too close to them, Phebe said that Jimmy was still very sick and it would just take time. The neighbors told Phebe that Caleb Fairchild, Phebe Aber and Sarah Mathias were still living but still very sick; that eleven other townspeople had died and many soldiers were dead. There appeared to be no let up to the sickness. Phebe learned also that General Washington was sick. He had a very bad sore throat and Mrs. Washington had arrived to take care of him. The General was in his bed at the tavern.

When Phebe returned she went to Jimmy's bedside. He was still sleeping but Phebe noticed that sores had appeared on his neck. She looked at his chest and saw more sores. Grandma Comfort was looking, too, and said, "This is the dangerous time. We have to watch these sores. If they start spreading and connecting to one another that's trouble. One good thing, there are none on his face. Look at the soles of his feet and see if there are any there."

Phebe lifted the blanket. "There aren't any, Comfort. Is that a good sign?"

"Yes," said Grandma Comfort, "Young boys like Jimmy have gone barefoot and the soles of their feet are toughened. I've heard that the pox can tear off the soles of tough feet. Let's hope these sores remain spread apart. All we can do is watch and wait. Thank goodness he sleeps."

Several more days passed. For Jimmy, the worst part of the pox was the itching. He itched all over. His mother and grandmother had to keep his hands tied down so he wouldn't scratch his skin off. For a day or so there had been no more sores appearing. Grandma Comfort said to Phebe, "I think the worst is over. Let's hope so."

There was a knock at the door. It was Jimmy's father, Joseph. Phebe talked with him but wouldn't let him come in. Grandma said the pox was still very catchable. Phebe asked how the boys were. Joseph said they were fine. They had no sign of the pox. Phebe told Joseph that Grandma thought the worst was over. Poor Joseph. He wanted to see Jimmy and talk to him but he understood why he couldn't and left to return home.

It was now over two weeks since Jimmy showed signs of smallpox. The worst was over but Jimmy still had to be careful for fear lung fever might get him. One afternoon there was a knock at the door. When Grandma Comfort answered, much to her surprise, she found General Washington there. "May I come in Mrs. Stiles? I would like to see Jimmy. I've had the pox before, so there is no chance I can catch it."

"Please come in, General. We are all honored to have you visit us. Jimmy is in the next room. Would you follow me?"

The General followed Grandma into the room where Phebe was sitting next to the bed. When she saw who the visitor was she was stunned. "General Washington, thank you for coming to see Jimmy." Jimmy was sleeping but his mother woke him to see his special visitor.

"Well, Jimmy, I hear you're over the worst of the pox. Now we are both veterans. I just came by to see how you are doing and to tell you that I miss having you as my aide. I've been sick, too, with quinsy, and Mrs. Washington came to take care of me. I've told her all about you and she looks forward to meeting you. Get rest and get well. I hope you will be back to work soon but don't rush it."

With that the General said goodbye and left.

The sores had cleared up and, though Jimmy had scars on his neck and chest, there were none on his face. He was now up and walking around the house but his mother wasn't going to let him go back to work for another week. Jimmy had another visitor. Phebe Aber and her mother came by. Phebe survived the pox, as Jimmy did, with no scars. The two were lucky. So did Sarah Mathias, but Caleb Fairchild's face was badly scarred.

Chapter Four

General Washington's Advice

Spring 1777

Spring finally came to Morristown. The pox still raged among the townspeople and the soldiers. Jimmy was no longer infectious and his father came to take him and his mother home. Joseph Stiles had tears in his eyes as he put his arms around his youngest son. Joseph helped his wife into the wagon and Jimmy sat between them on the ride home. As they rode away from Grandma Stiles' home, she warned Phebe not to let him do too much, too soon. Lung fever was still a danger especially in Jimmy's weakened condition.

The Stiles brothers, George, John and Joseph, decided to walk toward Morristown to meet their little brother. They hadn't seen their mother and Jimmy for almost two months and couldn't wait for the wagon to arrive. As they were walking past the Kemble farm, about a mile from their home, they saw in the distance a wagon approaching. The boys started to run toward it and George began to shout, "It's them! It's them!"

Within minutes the family was reunited. The little brother, who before was a pest to his older brothers, was now hugged by them. Joseph and Phebe looked on proudly. "We're very lucky, Joseph, very, very lucky. Jimmy has survived and George, John and Joseph didn't get the pox," said Phebe.

Jimmy rested for several weeks and then was back to normal. His mother couldn't keep him still any longer and he reported for work at the tavern as May began. Grandma Stiles insisted he stay with her rather than walk home at the end of every day. Since Grandpa's death she was lonely and liked to have Jimmy's company. At work, since the days were warmer, he didn't have to bring up as much firewood as before. The pox still raged on and poor Reverend Johnes had buried so many soldiers and so many of his parishioners that he looked worn and haggard and older than his sixty years. He could not have Sunday services in the church since it was still being used as a hospital. Instead, with the favorable spring weather, the townspeople met Sundays in the grove behind the Reverend's home. General Washington came frequently, bringing a camp chair with him and sitting at the rear of the congregation. Once, when Jimmy spent the weekend with Grandma Stiles, he and Grandma sat next to the great man.

Each morning Jimmy would saddle up his grandfather's horse and General Washington's horse and ride with the General to Loantika Valley as he inspected the soldiers encamped there. On one of the rides the General said, "Jimmy, very soon we will be leaving Morristown. I don't know if we will be back. You are much too young to come with me but I do have something I want you to do while I'm gone. I've talked to Colonel Hathaway about you and asked him to keep you active in the Morris Militia. Since that day in Springfield last December he thinks you are something special; that you have leadership qualities rarely found in a boy of thirteen. I'm afraid our problems with the British are not going to be over for some time and I want you to be ready. How much school have you had, Jimmy?"

"I went to school at a neighbor's house in New Vernon. I guess I was about six or seven when I started. I learned to read and do my numbers but I haven't been to school since I was eleven. I read pretty well and I'm very good with numbers."

"Your education was very much like mine, Jimmy. I left school when I was eleven, but while there, I learned to read very well and I was so good with my numbers that when I was still very young I became a surveyor. When my father was alive he sent my older brother to England to school but, when he died, my mother thought I could learn as much at a neighbor school. Knowing how to read became my education. Do you read a lot, Jimmy?"

"I read anything I can get my hands on, General, but that isn't much. I don't know anybody who has books."

"Well, Jimmy, before I leave Morristown I'm going to talk with Reverend Johnes and ask him if he can guide you in expanding your education. He is a good man, an educated man, and I know he will take you under his wing. Your neighbor, Peter Kemble, who lives near your home in New Vernon, has a very large library. I haven't met him but I'm sure Reverend Johnes knows him well enough to ask him to help you. Are you willing to work with Reverend Johnes?"

"Isn't Mr. Kemble a Tory, General? I've heard men talk about him at the tavern."

"Mr. Kemble is an old man, Jimmy. I know people think he is a Tory. He was quite close to the British five, maybe ten, years ago, but I don't think so now. From what I've heard in his age he doesn't remember much about the British. His daughter, Margaret, is married to General Thomas Gage of the British army, but his son, Richard, has taken the oath of allegiance to our cause. I don't think Mr. Kemble is any problem. Besides, all you want to do is borrow a few books to read. I don't think that will make any difference. Anyway, let Reverend Johnes worry about that. I am having dinner with Reverend Johnes tonight and I will speak to him about this. You didn't answer my question. Are you willing to work with the Reverend?"

"Yes, General, Thank you for your help. Although I like Mr. Arnold very much I don't think I want to sweep up the big room for the rest of my life," replied Jimmy.

"Jimmy, as I told you, I never had much school yet I think I'm as educated as many who have. Looking back, I think I learned most by watching and studying the people I knew. I paid special attention to the ones I respected but I also studied the ones I didn't. I was interested in avoiding their faults. So, the people you meet can be one of your most important schools. Watch them closely. Study them. One person I think you should study is Reverend Johnes. He is a special kind of man. Pay attention to him.

"Another school for you is the challenges you accept. That day in Springfield, when you stood firm with Colonel Hathaway, was one of those challenges. Before that, there was the challenge Colonel Ford gave you when you and your friends served as lookouts. You performed very well on both of those. We're living in a very stressful time, Jimmy, and I'm sure the opportunity for other such challenges will be many. Every time you perform well you will get more challenges and more opportunities to educate yourself. Never shirk from a challenge and you will never stop learning.

"Another school is what you read. Right now, that's where Reverend Johnes and Mr. Kemble can help."

They arrived at the Loantika campsite and General Washington went off to inspect the troops. Jimmy watered both the General's and Grandpa's horse at the brook that ran through the camp. The ride back to Morristown was quiet. General Washington rode ahead of Jimmy and talked with some of his aides. It was getting dark when they reached the Green and Jimmy noticed a crowd had gathered outside the tavern. They were soldiers in a different uniform than those already in Morristown.

Chapter Five

Colonel Morgan: A Study in Courage

Spring 1777

New troops had arrived. Their commander was at the tavern to report to General Washington. Jimmy noticed the man had an ugly scar on the side of his face. General Washington had warmly greeted the man and together they went upstairs to the General's office. The man, who seemed to be about the same age as the General, looked like he had been traveling for a long time. He was tired. It was plain the two men were close friends. The General sent a message downstairs to Mr. Arnold and asked for Jimmy to come to his office.

Jimmy went upstairs promptly and knocked at the General's door.

"Come in," ordered the General. "Jimmy, this is Colonel Daniel Morgan. He is an old friend of mine from the days of the French and Indian War. Colonel Morgan will be staying here for awhile and I want you to be his assistant as you are mine. Would you fix a tub of water for the Colonel and a room? As you can see he does need a bath and a little sleep won't hurt. Will it, Colonel?

47

"Thank you, General. I know I don't smell nice and I think I could sleep for a week. Hello, Jimmy, I'm glad to meet you," responded Colonel Morgan.

"I hope you have a pleasant stay with us at the tavern, Colonel. I'm here to help you any way I can. I'll go now and fix that tub."

Downstairs, Jimmy got out the tub and filled it half full with buckets of water from the rain barrel outside the tavern. Then he began pouring buckets of hot water that had been heating in the fireplace. The water was steaming as he poured it into the tub to heat up the bath water.

Colonel Morgan entered the room. "That tub looks good, Jimmy. Thank you for your help." The Colonel, with his back to Jimmy, took his shirt off. Jimmy gasped. The Colonel's back was a mass of scars. It looked as if someone once had sliced him over and over with a knife.

"I know I look awful, Jimmy. Between the scars on my back and the one on my face, I'm not exactly a pretty picture. You must be wondering what happened. Those scars are more than twenty years old. The one on my face came from being shot in the neck. I was a wagoner hauling supplies for General Braddock during his march to Fort Pitt. It was either a Frenchman or an Indian that did it. I don't know which. Anyway the bullet went in my neck and out my jaw taking a few teeth with it. I healed pretty fast but on the same trip I got into a fight with a British officer. I hit him with my fist and knocked him out. For punishment I was sentenced to receive a hundred whip lashes on the back. That tore my back to pieces as you can see. I counted each lash. I don't know how I stayed conscious but I did. They only whipped me ninety-nine times. I'm sure they miscounted 'cause I know they had no mercy. When I see my next British officer I'm going to remind him he owes me another lash, just before I shoot him. Now, you run along while I get clean. Where is my room?"

"Right though that door, Colonel. I'll make sure nobody bothers you. Have a good sleep."

Jimmy went upstairs to see if General Washington needed anything. He was working at the table looking at maps of the area. "Jimmy, did Colonel Morgan get his bath and his room?

"Yes, General, he is in the tub now and his room is right next to the tub room. Who is Colonel Morgan, General?"

"Jimmy, he is the best soldier I think I have ever met. I've known him since our days together with General Braddock in the war against the French and Indians. Colonel Morgan was born near where you live, over in Hunterdon. He ran away from home when he was very young. Couldn't get along with his father, I think. He might be a year or two younger than I am. He came to Virginia from New Jersey and became a wagoner. He was carrying supplies for General Braddock's expedition to Fort Pitt when I met him. Jimmy, Daniel Morgan is about the toughest man in the Continental Army. The reason he was so dirty is that he just arrived here after a long trip. He was captured, along with General Benedict Arnold, when they tried to take Quebec. They remained prisoners until they were exchanged for several British officers we had taken prisoner.

Jimmy asked, "Will Colonel Morgan be staying here?"

"Probably for several weeks. I've asked him to form a special fighting group to be added to the army. He's another person I think you should study. Watch him carefully, especially when he is leading his men. When you get a chance, look at that weapon of his. I don't think you've ever seen one quite like it before. It's a rifle, not a musket. Our soldiers are armed with muskets but a rifle is much more accurate than a musket and its range is much farther."

"Have you ever seen him fire it, General?" asked Jimmy.

"Yes, when I was in the Boston area Colonel Morgan, he was Captain Morgan then, joined our forces with a group of Virginians. They all had rifles. He gave a demonstration to General Charles Lee. General Lee heard Colonel Morgan say that he could shoot a squirrel in the head from three hundred yards with his rifle. The General challenged him to do so. Well, they couldn't find a squirrel but Morgan did hit a suitable target dead on from three hundred yards out. He told the General that each of his men could do the same.

"While Colonel Morgan is with us, Jimmy I want you to serve as his aide, just as you serve as mine. Watch him closely. Listen to him. He doesn't speak like a Harvard minister but his words are wise and absent of any nonsense. Watch especially how he treats and deals with men. That is what impresses me. That's what makes a leader."

Downstairs, Jimmy was sweeping the big room. One of the customers had just come from New Vernon and told Jimmy that his mother needed him at home to help with the garden so, instead of going to Grandma Stiles' house after work, he walked to New Vernon. The walk gave him time to think about General Washington's advice about how he might educate himself. It certainly made sense. Without going to school he could make his daily activities a real school. Study interesting people. Search out and accept challenges. Read good books. It seemed simple to do. Now, he had to do it. He thought Colonel Morgan, as General Washington said, was a man from whom he could learn much. He had to talk to Reverend Johnes about borrowing some books. But he didn't know how to create challenges that would help him grow. That would have to be left to chance.

He was in the garden working right after the sun came up. His older brothers were working with his father in the fields. He thought it would be easier working with his father and brothers because his mother had him on his knees weeding and the garden was big. Hours went by. It seemed he was not making any progress at all. As fast as he pulled weeds, more came up.

It took three days to weed the garden to his mother's satisfaction. He had to admit it was a fine looking garden. It was his mother's pride and joy. Finally, with the job completed, he was ready to go back to work at the tavern.

Chapter Six

A Visit with Reverend Timothy Johnes

Spring 1777

Jimmy was up bright and early the next morning and was on the road walking back to Morristown. As he approached the Green from the Vealtown Road he saw Reverend Johnes in the distance walking across the Green.

Coming closer Jimmy said politely, "Good morning, Reverend Johnes,"

"Good morning, Jimmy. I was just coming over to Mr. Arnold's to talk to you. The other evening General Washington came to our home for dinner. With all the things he has on his mind, you were the main topic of our dinner conversation. The General has taken a strong liking to you. He has no children of his own and I think he looks at you as if you were his son. He talked about how his early education and yours— you both stopped school when you were eleven years old—were similar. The General wanted me to prepare some books for you to read. What are your interests, Jimmy?"

'I don't know how to answer you, Reverend. Right now I have many interests, but I guess to you they are not important. I'm interested in animals. I love to look for beaver dams along the river. When I walk home and look to my right, I wonder where the hills came from. Since the soldiers came to Morristown I like to talk to them and find out where they come from and do they miss their home. I like to hear about the different places they have been. I'm so young I don't know what I'm interested in because I don't know about many things."

Reverend Johnes smiled. "Jimmy, now I see what General Washington sees in you. I've known your mother and father, your grandparents and great-grandparents. Being so close to your family and knowing you since you were born caused me to take you for granted. Or perhaps I overlooked the real you. Have you ever heard of John Locke, Jimmy?"

"No, Reverend. Is he from Morristown?"

"No. John Locke was an English writer. He's been dead for more than seventy years. What you just said, about not knowing what you are interested in because you don't know much yet, reminded me of something John Locke wrote. In one of his books he described the human mind as if it were a blank slate upon which knowledge is written. That knowledge gets there by what you experience. For example, before you saw your first beaver dam you had no knowledge of a beaver dam. Then when you saw one—when you experienced seeing a dam—that knowledge of what a beaver dam was like was written on that slate. With further observations and using your reason you have learned what you now know about beavers."

"Reverend, isn't that what General Washington was telling me to do--to educate myself? He told me to study people, to read books, to look for challenges and to accept them when they came."

"Exactly, Jimmy. What he wanted you to do is put yourself in a position where new things get written on that slate. Then by using your reason—your common sense—you come to an understanding. In fact, the book Locke wrote is called *An Essay on Human Understanding*."

"Is that one of the books you have, Reverend?"

"Yes, I have it. Do you have any books at home?

"The only book we have is the Bible, Reverend. That's how I taught myself to read. In fact, the Bible is the only book I ever held in my hands."

"Are there parts of the Bible you don't understand, Jimmy?"

"Lots of them, Reverend. When I don't understand something I ask my Ma or Pa what it means and they try to explain it. Sometimes that helps. Sometimes it doesn't."

"Jimmy, I'm sixty years old. I've read the Bible everyday of my adult life. I graduated from Yale University in 1737, was ordained a minister in 1743, and probably am one of the best educated citizens in New Jersey, but I have to admit there are many things in the Bible I don't understand. I still read and think and try to reason things out. Like you, I ask other people what they think something means. I never stop trying to understand. That's what you should do as well. Never stop trying to understand. I'm not going to loan you my copy of Locke's book on *Understanding*. Instead I'm going to loan you a different Locke book. It is on education and was written for a friend on how to teach his son. It's called *Some Thoughts Concerning Education*. It is easier to read than the essay. If you can understand this, maybe later you can try the essay. As you read, I want you to write down any word you don't know and anything you don't understand. Then we can discuss it later."

"I'll try it. This is going to be one of the challenges General Washington told me about, Reverend."

"It will be, Jimmy. Once a week, when you finish work and before you start for home I want to meet with you. I'm usually in the church at that time. Pick a day that is good for you and I'll make it a point to be at the church then. Would Monday be a good time?

"Monday is fine, Reverend. I'll come over to the church right after work," said Jimmy.

"So, next Monday we begin your education. Before you go see Mr. Arnold, I want you to walk with me across the Green. There is somebody I want you to meet. Do you know General Nathaniel Greene, Jimmy?"

"No, Reverend." said Jimmy. "I know who he is. I see him often with General Washington, but he has never spoken to me."

"I want you to meet him. He is a very interesting man and, in a way, very much like you. He never went to school. His father, a wealthy but very stern man, believed a boy

58

learned from work, not school and refused to let him attend school. His minister helped him, advised him, and loaned him books to read. In that way General Greene became well-educated. His minister is a relative of yours: Ezra Stiles. You probably never heard of him. Your grandfather, Captain Joseph, knew him. Reverend Stiles is now the President of Yale College."

Jimmy and Reverend Johnes walked across the Green to its opposite corner where General Greene's office was located. The general was inside looking at a map on a table with another man

"General Greene looked up. "Hello, Reverend Johnes. It's good to see you. What can I do for you?"

General Greene, a young man in his mid-thirties, walked toward the Reverend and Jimmy with his hand outstretched. Jimmy had seen him many times and noticed he walked with a limp.

"General, I want you to meet a young friend of mine. This is Jimmy Stiles. General Washington has taken a special interest in him and is very concerned that Jimmy gets a good education. I was telling Jimmy about your education."

"Hello, Jimmy. I've seen you over at Arnold's Tavern and General Washington has told me about you. He was very impressed with the courage you showed last winter at Springfield. I'm very pleased to meet you."

"I'm pleased to meet you too, General," answered Jimmy politely.

The General asked, "Jimmy, have you met Colonel Hamilton?"

"Yes, I have, General. I've done some chores for him over at the Tavern. Hello, Colonel Hamilton."

"Hello, Jimmy." Colonel Alexander Hamilton was an aide to General Washington. He didn't look much older than Jimmy.

Reverend Johnes said. "General, Jimmy is a relative of your friend, Reverend Ezra Stiles. Jimmy's great-grandfather came to Morristown years ago from Connecticut where he knew Reverend Stiles when he was a young man. I was hoping that you might spare a minute to tell Jimmy how you educated yourself through reading."

"Gladly, Reverend, but before I do I wonder if Jimmy would help me solve a problem. Your arrival with Jimmy gave me an idea. Colonel Hamilton and I think we have a spy in our midst. From what I have heard, Jimmy is very calm and steady when under stress and I could use those talents. Colonel Hamilton and I want to set a trap for this spy and Jimmy can help us. Will you help us, Jimmy?"

Jimmy answered eagerly, "Of course, General Greene. What do I have to do?"

"I'll explain." said General Greene.

"Before you do, General," interrupted Reverend Johnes, "I'm going to leave Jimmy with you and return to the church. When you two are finished, send Jimmy over to the church. I have a book for him."

"I will, Reverend, and I will have that talk with Jimmy about his education. Thank you for bringing him here."

Reverend Johnes left the office and began his walk across the Green to the church.

Chapter Seven

Jimmy Helps Catch a Spy

Spring 1777

General Greene directed Jimmy to a table in the corner of the room and told him to sit down. Colonel Hamilton and General Greene both sat down with him. Colonel Hamilton spoke: "Jimmy, do you know Jonas Van Dyken?"

"I know who he is, Colonel. I've seen him many times at the tavern," answered Jimmy.

Colonel Hamilton explained, "Mr. Van Dyken is the man we suspect of being a spy. He is able to pass through the British lines and get into New York City and we have been using him as a spy for us, but we think he is a double spy."

"What is a double spy?" asked Jimmy.

General Greene answered, "A double spy is a person who is spying for both sides. Usually a person like that is paid money for his spying. Since we were not paying Van Dyken, we thought he was helping us out for patriotic reasons. But lately, the British have had information about our plans they could only have received from Van Dyken. The problem is we aren't sure. Benoni Hathaway, your colonel, told me about you finding the gunpowder mill while looking for beaver and how Colonel Ford swore you into the militia and to secrecy about the mill. Colonel Hathaway also told me how you reported hearing a group of men talking at the tavern about the mill. When you reported that conversation to him, he passed that information on to General Washington's headquarters and we alerted a spy in New York to be on the watch for any information about the mill. When you and your friends spotted the signal that the British troops were coming, the militia was able to stop them at Springfield last January. Now, Jimmy, we need your help again. Colonel Hamilton has a plan that he will explain to you."

Colonel Alexander Hamilton began, "Jimmy, tomorrow afternoon Van Dyken will be here to give us a report on what he has learned in New York. Like so much of his information, his report will be of little value to us. He tells us only so much as to make us think he is useful. When he arrives, I'm going to send someone over to the tavern to get you. Come here with your broom. You are to make Van Dyken think no one is watching him. I will leave fake papers on the map table with information about our troop strength. It is false information and makes us seem much stronger than we really are. If Van Dyken is the spy we think he is, the temptation will be too great and he will steal these papers. I want you to be a witness to the theft. I'm hoping he won't suspect you so you are going to have to act like a disinterested sweeper. I'm going to be out of the room for a few minutes and this will give time for Van Dyken to hide the papers in his coat. Do you think you can do this?"

"I sure can," answered Jimmy, "This is going to be fun."

"Good," said Colonel Hamilton. "Now, I want to hear what General Greene has to say about your schooling."

"Jimmy," General Greene began, "I can say what I have to say quickly. I know that going to a school is out of the question for you. I didn't go to school because my father had no faith in schools. He was wrong, but I had to make the best of what was given me. Your relative, Reverend Ezra Stiles, was to me what Reverend Johnes is to you. Listen to him and do what he says. General Washington told me what he told you about reading good books and he told me about telling you to watch closely and imitate people you respect and to take advantage of opportunities where you can be challenged. One such opportunity will be what you are doing tomorrow to help us find the spy. You are on the right track. Jimmy, stay close to Reverend Johnes. He is one of those great people General Washington told you about.

"Now, Jimmy, go back to Reverend Johnes at the church. I'll send for you tomorrow afternoon. Oh yes, don't forget your broom."

Jimmy crossed back across the Green. Reverend Johnes was waiting in the church for him. He had the book that he wanted Jimmy to read.

That night Jimmy stayed at Grandma Stiles' home. Although it was mid-May Grandma had some logs burning in the fireplace to take the chill off the house. Jimmy lay in front of the fire and began to read. Reverend Johnes was right. It was hard, but he did as Reverend Johnes told him and wrote down the words he didn't know. It was slow-going and soon his eyes began to droop. Grandma chased him off to bed.

It was early in the afternoon of the next day when a soldier came into the tavern and asked to see Jimmy. When Jimmy came into the room the soldier told him, "Colonel Hamilton would like to see you. The colonel said not to forget your broom. You would know why."

Jimmy told Mr. Arnold where he was going, grabbed his broom and started across the Green. When he came into General Greene's office Colonel Hamilton was there talking with Jonas Van Dyken. Both men ignored Jimmy when he entered and he went right to work sweeping the floor. In a minute or so he overheard Colonel Hamilton tell Van Dyken that he had to leave for a few minutes and saw him leave the room. Jimmy continued sweeping and acted as if he was concentrating on the broom but he was keeping an eye on Van Dyken. Van Dyken was looking at the papers Colonel Hamilton had left on the table. He made a quick glance at Jimmy and satisfied that Jimmy was not paying attention to him, quickly snatched the papers and put them inside his coat. Jimmy pretended he didn't see a thing and kept busy sweeping. In a few minutes Colonel Hamilton returned and resumed his conversation with Van Dyken. Several minutes later Van Dyken left and General Greene entered the room.

"Well. Jimmy," asked Colonel Hamilton. "Did Van Dyken take our bait?"

"He sure did." responded Jimmy. "You no sooner left the room and he was reading your papers. As soon as he realized what they were he put them in his coat."

"Did he wait until you were looking away before he took the papers?" asked General Greene.

"No, he glanced at me and just ignored me. I think he thought a boy with a broom was just part of the room's furniture."

General Greene reached over and patted Jimmy on the shoulder. "You did a good job, Jimmy. I now know what General Washington sees in you. I'm sure the British will have the stolen papers in their hands by tomorrow and Jonas Van Dyken will think how smart he is.

"Thank you, Jimmy. You performed magnificently. I can't wait to tell General Washington what a great actor you are."

Chapter Eight

Colonel Daniel Morgan: A Study in Leadership

May 1777

The next day Jacob Arnold was waiting for Jimmy when he came to work. "Jimmy, General Washington wants you to stay with Colonel Morgan today. I don't know what the Colonel is planning to do but stay with him and help in any way you can."

"Yes, Mr. Arnold. I think I know what the General wants me to do," responded Jimmy.

Jimmy went out the front door of the tavern and walked over to the Green where Colonel Morgan was speaking to a group of soldiers. "You men have been with me since we left Virginia two years ago. We've been through hard times together. We marched together from Maine to Quebec in the winter. We have known victory and we have suffered defeat. What is facing us now will be harder than anything we have ever been through before. I want you to know how much faith I have in you. I will go anywhere with you men. General Washington has asked me to form a group of fighters—a special force. He wants this force to be a model for other soldiers to copy. He wants men who are

68

excellent shots, men who are hardened veterans, men who don't mind hardship, men who can face death and still perform their duty without hesitation. You are that kind of men and I want you to go among the regiments here in Morristown and select men who, in your opinion, could be the kind of soldiers you are. General Washington wants five hundred men in this special force. They will be called Rangers, just as we are. That means each of you will select ten men. I don't know if you can find that many, but give it a try."

A tall, rugged looking man spoke out, "Colonel, when do we get started and where do we find these regiments?"

"Right now. We're going over to Loantika Valley this morning. It's about three miles from here. There are some soldiers there who don't believe what they've heard about your marksmanship. We're going to give them a demonstration of what Rangers can do before making our choices. Let's go."

Carrying his rifle at his side, Colonel Morgan began running. The men followed. If Jimmy wanted to stay with the Colonel he had to run, too. The Colonel set a fast pace; the men stayed right with him, and Jimmy had to keep up.

After they had run about a mile Jimmy hoped they would take a rest, but they kept going. Colonel Morgan, without saying a word, was leading. The men stayed with him. Jimmy's legs began to get heavy and he was breathing rapidly, but Colonel Morgan kept up the steady pace. Jimmy thought he had to stop to rest but he knew if he did, Colonel Morgan and the men would leave him. From somewhere, as if in a dream, came General Washington's voice, "This is a challenge, Jimmy." Jimmy forgot the pain and kept going.

Colonel Morgan and his Rangers were singing what sounded like an Indian song when they arrived at Loantika. Jimmy had never heard it before. When they stopped running Jimmy sat down under a tree to catch his breath. Colonel Morgan and the Rangers looked like they had just taken a short walk. Right then, Jimmy decided he was not going to walk home to New Vernon any more. He was going to run.

Colonel Morgan was over six feet tall and weighed over two hundred pounds. The Rangers with him were all over six feet and everyone looked as if he could beat any Redcoat he met. They were dressed alike. Each wore a round wool hat, a hunting shirt, breeches, leather leggings

70

and Indian moccasins. Across their chests they had sewn their motto in capital letters— "LIBERTY OR DEATH." Their arrival at Loantika caused a flurry of excitement and men from many regiments came to see the new arrivals. They were especially interested in their rifles. Most soldiers in the camp carried muskets. Many had never seen a rifle and wanted to see it fired. Colonel Morgan said to the Loantika soldiers looking on, "Come over here men. I'll show you how these rifles can fire." He gave his hat to one of the Rangers and told him to go out about three hundred yards and attach the hat to a tree. Then he showed the Loantika soldiers how to load the rifle. The soldiers laughed and said the rifle took too long to load, but when the Colonel fired at the hat and they saw that he hit it, their laughter stopped. One by one the Colonel's men stepped up and fired. Everyone hit the hat. The hat wasn't much good after the shooting but the Loantika soldiers were impressed.

Colonel Morgan explained, "Yes, a musket can be fired more rapidly than our long rifles, but our long rifles are many times more accurate. You see, a musket has a smooth bore; a rifle has spiral grooves in the barrel. The grooves put a spin on the bullet which make it go farther and give it more accuracy. When you pack a bullet into a smooth bore it goes in faster. With the rifles grooves it takes longer. If I had Redcoats coming at me at a close distance I'd want a musket in my hands. But when the British are farther away, when they can't hit me, but I can hit them, I want a long rifle. Wouldn't you?"

The soldiers listening to Colonel Morgan paid close attention to what he was saying. He did not speak very long and finally said. "If any of you wish to join our group or learn more about us gather over there under that tree where the boy is.

Jimmy was surprised at the number of men who came over to the tree where he was standing. There had to be more than five hundred. Colonel Morgan directed that they break up into groups of ten to twenty and then assigned one or two Rangers to each group. They would answer the soldiers' questions and select those soldiers they thought could become Rangers.

General Washington had given orders that those soldiers who wished to serve with Colonel Morgan would be released by their commanding officers. At the end of the day over four hundred men had joined Morgan's Rangers.

Jimmy had listened to Colonel Morgan talk and wondered what General Washington would want him to notice about the man. What could he learn from Colonel Morgan? He did not speak well. He did not have a loud voice. He was not taller or bigger than his Rangers. He dressed just like them. Yet, for some reason he stood out above them all. Jimmy noticed that the Colonel did not tell the men how to use the rifle or how to attack an enemy; he showed them. You sensed the respect the Rangers and soldiers had for him. You knew he was the leader. Jimmy wondered if Colonel Morgan had something he could imitate or was it something you either had or didn't have. He had to ask General Washington and Reverend Johnes that question.

In late afternoon Colonel Morgan called Jimmy over to him and told him that he was staying the night with his men at Loantika. He instructed Jimmy to go back to Morristown and wait for further instructions from General Washington. Jimmy started the walk back to town but then decided he was going to be a Ranger. He started to run. He set his own pace and found the running enjoyable. In time he knew his legs would get more and more used to running wherever he wanted to go.

Chapter Nine

The Army leaves Morristown

June 1777

When Jimmy arrived at Arnold's Tavern the next day there was a flurry of activity. The American army was leaving Morristown. Amidst all the hustle and bustle General Washington called Jimmy to his office.

"Jimmy, I can only spare a moment, but before I leave I want to make sure you will work hard to do those things I told you to do about teaching yourself."

"I will, General Washington. I promise," replied Jimmy. "Will you be coming back to Morristown, General?"

"I don't know, Jimmy. The answer to that question depends on what the British do. I hope someday to return to Morristown if only to see you. I must leave now, Jimmy. Keep your promise."

"I will, General Washington," said Jimmy.

Within a day the soldiers, who filled the streets, homes and outbuildings of Morristown and vicinity, were gone. They marched off as quietly as they arrived on the same roads that brought them to Morristown. Only a few were left behind to protect the powder mill and man the lookout posts. Jimmy returned to his work at the tavern but he missed the excitement when General Washington lived there. He wished he could have gone with the soldiers wherever they were going.

Summer came to Morristown and Jimmy was busy doing chores for Mr. Arnold. Every few days he would go home. Before, he used to walk the road to Basking Ridge, now he ran all the way. He was practicing to be a Ranger with Colonel Morgan. By August Jimmy found that his legs had grown stronger, that he could run to Morristown faster and faster. Some of the old timers that came to the tavern began to call him "Running Deer." He liked the name.

At the tavern, while waiting on customers, Jimmy heard bits and pieces of what was going on with the soldiers. He learned that General Washington and the army were heading for Philadelphia to prevent the British from taking the city. He learned later some bad news. The army had been defeated at a place called Brandywine, again at Germantown, and forced to leave Philadelphia in British control.

In October a group of soldiers came into the tavern. They had just arrived in Morristown after a trip from Peekskill and were very happy. They brought great news of an American victory at Saratoga, New York. Jimmy's ears perked up when he heard one of them mention Daniel Morgan and his Rangers and how they had helped bring about the defeat of General John Burgoyne. As news of the victory spread around town people gathered at the tavern to learn more about the battle and to celebrate.

By November the happy mood in Morristown had changed. The news from General Washington's army was not good. The British had pushed the army out of Philadelphia to a line about twenty miles further west. With winter coming, the townspeople wondered where the camp would be.

The first snow had fallen in late November and the Green was still covered in white a week later. Jimmy had been at home with his mother and father for several days and when he returned to Morristown on December 2 he saw that a crowd had gathered on the Green across from the tavern.

Jimmy's friend, Caleb Fairchild, was standing at the edge of the crowd. Caleb was one of the lookouts who stood watch at the top of Kinney's Hill a year ago. Like Jimmy, Caleb had survived the pox but his face had been terribly scarred and he wore a woolen cloth to cover the scars.

"Caleb, what is going on?" asked Jimmy.

"Jimmy, they're going to hang people today. See the scaffold over there?

"What people?

"They brought a lot of people in from Princeton yesterday and put them over in the courthouse. Pretty soon they are going to start the hanging," answered Caleb.

"What did they do? Why do they want to hang them?

"They're Tories, Jimmy. I hear they're spies."

"Wait here, Caleb. I'm going inside and ask Mr. Arnold. He'll know."

Jimmy left Caleb on the edge of the Green and crossed over to the tavern. Mr. Arnold was just inside the door looking out a window. Reverend Johnes was standing with him.

"Good morning, Jimmy. You got back just in time for all the excitement, I see", said Mr. Arnold.

"Good morning, Reverend Johnes. Good morning, Mr. Arnold. What's going on, Mr. Arnold? Caleb Fairchild said there was going to be a hanging."

"Caleb's right, Jimmy. The Council of Safety has been meeting in Princeton and sentenced thirty-five men to death for treason. They had been enlisting New Jersey residents in the British army. They were tried, sentenced to death and sent to Morristown to be kept in the County Jail until the date of their execution. Today is the day," said Mr. Arnold.

Jimmy was astounded. "You mean," Jimmy asked, "thirty-five men are going to be hanged today? Right here on the Green?"

'I'm afraid so, Jimmy. Unless some of them volunteer to join the Continental Army, they're all going to die today. I take that back. Two of them don't get a choice. I guess they are the worst of the lot. One is named Jim Iliff, the other, Johnny Mee. I don't know either of them. They aren't from around here. Those two are going to be hanged, for sure," said Mr. Arnold.

Reverend Johnes spoke, "Jimmy, I want you to busy yourself with whatever Mr. Arnold wants you to do around here. I don't think you should join the crowd outside and watch this hanging.   This is serious business. It is not entertainment. You are only thirteen and it is something I don't want you to see. Do you understand?"

"Yes, Reverend. I don't want to watch it. I have to go outside to tell Caleb Fairchild. I don't think he'll want to see it either."

Later in the day Jimmy heard the crowd outside give a cheer. He went to Mr. Arnold and asked, "Is it over, Mr. Arnold?"

"Yes, Jimmy. It is. They only hanged the two. The rest agreed to join the army and saved their lives. Reverend Johnes said he wanted to talk to you before you went to your Grandma's house. He is over at the church."

Jimmy walked across the Green to the Church. The crowd was gone, the Green was quiet, but the scaffold was still there as a reminder of what happened. Reverend Johnes was inside the Church putting new candles in their holders along one side.

"Hello, Jimmy," he said. "You finished your chores early. Will you help me replace these used candles? We can talk while we work."

Jimmy right away began removing the candles from the holders. He had helped Reverend Johnes before and knew just what to do. As Reverend Johnes and Jimmy worked they talked.

"Jimmy, I didn't want you to see the hanging today. It wasn't because I wanted to protect you from seeing death. You've seen death. You saw your Grandfather die. Several of your best friends died from smallpox. You faced death that day with Colonel Hathaway in Springfield. I didn't want you to be part of that grizzly affair on the Green. The execution was becoming a sporting event. I didn't want you to think the way that crowd acted was normal behavior. People cheer at a horse race. not when someone dies at a public hanging. Most of the people in that crowd were people you and I know. I felt you didn't need that memory in your young mind."

"I'm glad I didn't see it, Reverend. Why did they have to hang them?" asked Jimmy.

"Since that day at Lexington and Concord," explained the Reverend, "we have been at war. War is not nice, Jimmy, but we will not be an independent country by turning our cheek to the Redcoats. We tried to talk to them and that didn't work. So it came to war and we, living in Morristown, are right in the middle of it. The two men hanged today were found guilty of enlisting young men into the British army. They were colonials. They weren't British soldiers. So, to the court in Princeton, where they were tried, they were guilty of treason. Those other men, who were also to be hanged, were found guilty of treason for joining the British army. They were given a chance to live if they joined the colonial army. The other two weren't."

"Reverend, do you think the two men would have changed their minds if they were given a choice?" asked Jimmy.

"I don't know. I talked to them before they died. I was there on the gallows with them when Sheriff Carmichael asked if they wanted to confess to their crime. The two men looked at each other, and shook their heads no. Jim Iliff, the older one, said, 'The only thing we're guilty of is loyalty to our King. We have no confession to make.'"

"They sounded like brave men to me," responded Jimmy. "They might have been found guilty of treason, and maybe the hanging was a just punishment, but I don't think I could have faced hanging as bravely as they did."

"I hope you never have to find out, Jimmy." said Reverend Johnes. "I heard a story recently about a family my wife's sister knew. She lived near the family in Coventry, Connecticut. Their name was Hale and their son was hanged by the British in New York City last September. The son, Nathan, was twenty-two years old. General Washington and the army had just retreated from Manhattan Island and were near White Plains. The General needed information about the size, strength, and location of the British and asked for volunteers who would sneak through the British lines and get that information. Young Hale volunteered to go. He was told that if the British caught him he would be hanged as a spy, but he went anyway. The British did catch him and, without a trial, sentenced him to death. When Nathan was asked if he had any final words, he said, 'I only regret that I have but one life to lose for my country.' When Iliff made his statement just before he was hanged it reminded me of what young Hale had said. Jimmy, this world is full of many cowards. Nathan Hale was not one. And, even though they worked for the British, Mee and Iliff weren't cowards either. Why did they have to hang them? We are in a war, Jimmy, and war is a terrible thing and terrible things happen."

Jimmy and Reverend Johnes finished replacing the candles. Reverend Johnes thanked him for helping and Jimmy went home to Grandma Stiles' house.

Chapter Ten

Valley Forge

The Winter of 1778

A light snow blew in Jimmy's face as he walked from Grandma Stiles' house to the Green and Arnold's Tavern. It was now early February and Jimmy didn't look forward to his run home to New Vernon after work. About mid-morning Mr. Arnold sent him on an errand to the other side of the Green. On his way he met Aunt Rachel, his Uncle John's widow. Uncle John, Grandpa Stiles' younger brother, died the previous May from the pox and Jimmy hadn't seen Aunt Rachel since the funeral. She lived a few miles from Morristown in Hanover Neck.

"Hello, Aunt Rachel. It's good to see you. How is Cousin Job? I haven't seen him since the army left." Cousin Job was five years older than Jimmy and had joined the army last spring.

"He's home in Hanover Neck, Jimmy. He was sent home to gather up supplies—food, blankets and clothing-- for the army. Jimmy, Job is sick. Bad sick. He's got scabies and chest fever. If he goes back to the army with those supplies I know he will die. I've come to town to talk to Grandma Stiles and ask her for her advice."

"What is scabies, Aunt Rachel? I never heard of that," asked Jimmy.

"It's sores and itches all over your body. It comes from being dirty and living in filth. Job tells me the whole army has it. You catch it very easily and it spreads all over. The soldiers all have bugs and lice. The living conditions are terrible. The soldiers are sick, starving and freezing

"Where is the army, Aunt Rachel?" asked Jimmy.

"They are in a place called Valley Forge. It's about twenty miles from Philadelphia but very difficult to get to because the British have patrols all over to prevent supplies from getting there. Job says you have to go to Easton, Pennsylvania and then west before turning south or else the British patrols will get you. On such a trip I don't think Job would last more than two or three days the way he is now."

"Aunt Rachel, I have to run an errand for Mr. Arnold. I'll meet you back at Grandma's house as quickly as I can."

Jimmy completed his errand and rushed back to the tavern where he went to Mr. Arnold and told him what Aunt Rachel had just said. Mr. Arnold instructed Jimmy to run to Mr. Hathaway's house and ask him to come to the tavern right away.

Benoni Hathaway's home was about a quarter mile from the tavern on the side of a hill that dropped into the hollow of Morristown. Jimmy delivered the message to Mr. Hathaway and also told him what Aunt Rachel had said. Mr. Hathaway instructed Jimmy to go immediately to Grandma Stiles' home and have Aunt Rachel stay there until Mr. Arnold and Mr. Hathaway arrived.

Jimmy did as he was told and, with Grandma Stiles and Aunt Rachel ,waited for the two men to come. Within half an hour they came to the house and Aunt Rachel told them what Job's instructions were.

Benoni Hathaway was the commander of the Morris County Militia. He told Aunt Rachel to go home and not let Job return to his unit until he was healthy. He told her to also tell him not to worry about his orders to return to Valley Forge with supplies because the militia would gather the supplies and deliver them to the army.

With that, Mr. Hathaway and Mr. Arnold left. Grandma Stiles told Aunt Rachel that it would be better if she could bring Job to her house where she could help Aunt Rachel care for him. Aunt Rachel agreed and said she would return with Job as soon as she could. Jimmy hitched the horse to the wagon and gave it to Aunt Rachel to return to Hanover Neck and bring Job back. He rode with her to the Green and then went to the tavern.

Meanwhile, Benoni Hathaway readied the cannon on the Green and fired three shots—the signal to the militia in the area to gather at the Green. Within an hour about thirty men arrived and as time passed more came. Colonel Hathaway spoke to the group and told them about Job's orders and explained that he wanted them to spread out in the area and alert the people to the problem at Valley Forge.

Within two days the Green was jammed with wagons full of clothing and food. Men and women were busy sorting the goods and packing the wagons preparing the caravan for a quick departure to Valley Forge. Benoni Hathaway was in command of all the activity and was busy selecting people who would travel to Valley Forge. He could not use the militia. They were needed to protect Morristown and the very important powder mill. The British forces on Staten Island were only a day and a half march from Morristown. Many older men volunteered to drive the wagons and Jimmy asked his grandmother for permission to go. She told him she could not give him permission. Only his mother and father could. So Jimmy told Mr. Arnold he had to go home and started running for Basking Ridge. He was home by noon, asked his mother and father, and they both agreed to let him go. He had something to eat and was on the road again for Morristown.

On his return to the Green, Jimmy sought out Mr. Hathaway and told him he had his mother and father's permission to go with the caravan. Mr. Hathaway was pleased and accepted Jimmy's offer to go.

"Jimmy, the caravan will be leaving tomorrow morning. Go home to your Grandma's and gather up some warm clothes and take a warm pair of boots. I'll see you early tomorrow morning."

When Jimmy arrived at his Grandma's house, Aunt Rachel and Job were there. The two women were putting Job in bed. He looked sick. He had told Aunt Rachel that he had come to

Morristown from Valley Forge by way of Easton, Pennsylvania and that the supplies should go to Valley Forge by the same route. She had left a message at Arnold's Tavern for Colonel Hathaway telling him what Job had said.

The next morning, when Jimmy arrived at the Green, he learned that Colonel Hathaway had appointed Elijah Freeman to lead the caravan. Mr. Freeman was from Mendham and had a brother living in Easton, Pennsylvania. The brother knew how to get to Valley Forge. Mr. Freeman was also an expert wagoner and knew how to manage a wagon train.

The caravan would have seventeen wagons and Mr. Freeman was busy making sure the wagons were properly loaded. He didn't want too heavy a load in any one wagon. The most important part of the caravan was the horses and the skilled teamster didn't want to over work them.

At mid-morning they left the Green and headed toward Mendham. Jimmy was assigned to the third wagon. Everyone except the drivers walked beside the wagons. Thankfully, there was no snow on the ground. The first stop was in Mendham. The horses rested and were given some water. By mid-afternoon the caravan had reached Black River. There they rested again before moving on to German Valley where they arrived after nightfall and spent the night. Jimmy's wagon was loaded with clothes and blankets and he buried himself under them and slept very well. Keeping the Musconetcong Mountains to the right, Elijah Freeman led the wagon train westward through the valley

By the end of the third day the caravan had reached the Delaware River across from Easton. There they had to wait to be ferried across. Mr. Freeman explained where he was going to Mr. Martin, the owner of the ferry, who quickly agreed to ferry the whole caravan across if word was given to General Washington of Mr. Martin's contribution to the cause of the revolution. Elijah Freeman introduced Jimmy to Mr. Martin telling him that Jimmy was very close to General Washington and would tell him of Mr. Martin's patriotism. With that, the deal was made and the first wagon was loaded on to a raft.

Jimmy watched fascinated. Two heavy ropes had been stretched across the river about twenty feet above the water. They were guide ropes for the raft. Two ropes extended from the guide ropes and were attached to the raft. These ropes slid along the guide ropes on a leather collar greased with pig fat. They were to prevent the raft from going down river with the current. Another rope was attached to the front of the raft and another to the rear. A team of horses on the Pennsylvania side of the river were to pull that rope and haul the raft across. On the return trip a team on the New Jersey side would haul the raft back.

It took all day for the seventeen wagons to cross. Jimmy watched each crossing. That evening it began to rain. The wagons were covered and Jimmy slept on the floor of Bachmann's Tavern in Easton.

The next day they traveled west to Northhampton, spent the night there and turned south. Their destination was an iron forge belonging to the Potts family. It took two days to reach Potts' Forge. There they learned they were about twenty miles from the army encampment at Valley Forge, another forge in this iron-rich area. Mr. Freeman learned that General Washington's headquarters was in a home owned by a relative of the family that owned Potts' Forge.

So far, the weather had been good. There were brief periods of snow but not enough to really hamper the caravan. The horses were in good condition thanks to Mr. Freeman's skill.

Two days later, very early in the morning, the caravan arrived at the outer limits of the Valley Forge encampment. The sights stunned Jimmy. He knew things were bad from what Aunt Rachel told him, but he didn't imagine it was as bad as it was. It seemed that everyone he saw was sick. Mr. Freeman asked where the headquarters was located and one of the soldiers volunteered to lead the wagon train there. They had to ford a stream and on the other side was a large stone house with several outbuildings. The wagon train stopped and Mr. Freeman walked to the stone house. He took Jimmy with him in case they ran into General Washington.

Inside was a beehive of activity. Jimmy spotted Colonel Hamilton sitting at a table with a pile of papers in front. Several other officers were standing beside the table. Jimmy approached and Colonel Hamilton looked up,

"Jimmy Stiles! What are you doing here?" he asked.

"I just arrived with a wagon train of clothing and food from Morristown, Colonel. Do you remember Mr. Freeman? He's our wagon train leader and needs to know what we should do with the supplies."

"God bless the people of Morris!" exclaimed Colonel Hamilton. "Of course, I remember Mr. Freeman. He was a leader in the militia. Good to see you again, Elijah. Major Tomkins, please get someone to show these people where to take their wagons."

Colonel Hamilton stood up to shake Mr. Freeman's hand and said, "Elijah, thank you for coming so far. Our soldiers need those supplies badly. I just hope we can make it through this winter. Elijah and Jimmy, come with me. There is someone in the next room who would like to see you."

Jimmy and Mr. Freeman followed Colonel Hamilton into another room. There was General Washington and General Greene talking with a rather stern looking man. The General looked up and immediately broke into a smile as he recognized Jimmy.

'Oh, my goodness! Jimmy! It's so good to see you."

"Good morning, General," responded Jimmy looking at General Washington's face and thinking how tired he looked. "We just arrived from Morristown with seventeen supply wagons for the army. It isn't much for so many men."

"Jimmy, every little bit helps. Other towns from Delaware, New Jersey and Pennsylvania are all helping out. If the soldiers can last just a little bit longer, maybe we might make it through this winter."

Turning to Mr. Freeman, General Washington said, "Elijah, it's good to see you again. How are Benoni Hathaway and Mr. Arnold I miss them and all the good people of Morristown." Looking at the man standing next to him, the General said, "I want you to meet Baron von Steuben. He just arrived here from Paris and has come to help us. The Baron is an expert in training soldiers and we certainly need his help."

Jimmy and Mr. Freeman both greeted the Baron. Mr. Freeman spoke to General Washington, "General, Colonel Hathaway instructed me to tell you that he is keeping Private Job Stiles in Morristown because he is too sick to travel back to the army. He was under orders to gather supplies and return to Valley Forge. We did that for him. Colonel Hathaway will send him back to duty as soon as he is able to travel. Job is Jimmy's cousin."

"I understand," responded the General. "I will write an order for you to give to Benoni explaining what he should do with Job."

Mr. Freeman continued, "General, when we crossed the Delaware River at Easton, when we needed a ferry, a Mr. John Martin ferried our seventeen wagons across the river—one at a time—and did it for free. He asked only that we bring his contribution to our cause to your attention."

The General immediately went to his desk and quickly wrote a message and handed it to Mr. Freeman instructing him to give it to Mr. Martin on the return trip. Then, turning to Jimmy he said, "Before you return to Morristown I want to speak to you. Tell Colonel Hamilton and he will bring you right in."

"Yes, General Washington," answered Jimmy.

Mr. Freeman spoke, "General, we will be leaving the first thing in the morning. We have to get the wagons unloaded now and give the horses a rest. It was good to see you again, sir."

Major Tomkins directed Mr. Freeman to where he could deliver the supplies. Jimmy and Mr. Freeman returned to the wagon train. By

95

mid-afternoon the wagons were emptied, the horses were watered and sheltered in lean-tos next to the Potts' barn.

Early the next morning the lead wagon of the Morristown caravan, with Mr. Freeman at the reins and Jimmy Stiles sitting beside him, pulled up in front of the headquarters. Jimmy jumped down and entered the building. Colonel Hamilton was there and immediately took him in to see General Washington.

"Good morning, Jimmy" said General Washington. "I have a letter for you to take home to Reverend Johnes. There is also an essay by Thomas Paine I would like him to read to the people of Morristown. You will never know how much the loyalty and sacrifice of those people means to me and to the soldiers. As for you, Jimmy, I want you to tell Colonel Hathaway and the people of Morristown that when spring arrives and the army regains its strength we hope to continue the war against the British. If this brings us back into New Jersey, ask the Colonel to be ready with his militia to join with us."

"I will, General," promised Jimmy.

The General continued, "I hope you are keeping up with your reading and following

Reverend Johnes' advice. Coming here with Mr. Freeman and the wagon train is evidence that you are accepting those challenges I told you about. I am very proud of you, Jimmy. Have a safe trip home."

"Thank you, General Washington. Good-bye."

Chapter Eleven

The Return to Morristown

Winter 1778

With the wagons empty the caravan moved more rapidly on the return trip to Morristown. At Easton Mr. Freeman found Mr. Martin and gave him the note that General Washington had written. As Mr. Martin read it, tears came to his eyes and he turned to Mr. Freeman and said, "I shall treasure this for the rest of my days. Thank you very much." He gave the note to Mr. Freeman to read, *"Dear Mr. Martin, Mr. Elijah Freeman told me of the assistance you gave him as his wagon train bringing supplies to the army here at Valley Forge crossed the Delaware River. Please know that I and my soldiers are very grateful for your service to us and our country's cause. Thank you,*

General George Washington."

Two days later, just before dusk, they reached the Green. Jimmy jumped off the lead wagon and went immediately to the church where he delivered General Washington's letter to Reverend Johnes. Afterwards, he went to Grandma Stiles and learned that Job's health was much improved and that he had returned to Valley Forge and his unit.

The next Sunday Reverend Johnes' sermon was about the General's letter. He read the letter to the congregation; it was very short thanking the people of the Morristown area for their loyalty and sacrifice. Reverend Johnes went on to talk about the essay of Thomas Paine that General Washington had also sent to him. He explained that it had been written last September, just after the defeat at the battle of Brandywine. The Reverend told the congregation that General Washington had underlined several passages in the essay and then began to read one of the underlined passages:

"There are many men who will do their duty when it is not wanted, but a genuine public spirit always appears most when there is most occasion for it. Thank God! Our army, though fatigued, is yet entire....I have seen them in circumstances a thousand times more trying than the present. It is only those that are not in action, that feel languor and heaviness, and the best way to rub it off is to turn out, and make sure work of it....We fight not to enslave, but to set a country free, and to make room upon the earth for honest men to live in. In such a case we are sure that we are right."

Reverend Johnes looked up from reading the essay and told the congregation that since Thomas Paine had written that essay the army had gone into winter quarters at Valley Forge and said, "We have with us today someone who has just returned from Valley Forge. He and other members of our congregation were with the wagon train that took supplies there. I single this person out for two reasons: One, he is not yet fourteen years old. Two, General Washington asked me to assist in his education by putting him into challenging situations. Having just completed one challenging situation, the trip to Valley Forge, I now am going to put him into another challenging situation. Jimmy Stiles, please come forward and tell the congregation what you saw at Valley Forge."

Jimmy was sitting in the left balcony of the church and was startled when he heard Reverend Johnes mention his name. He looked down at Grandma Stiles and saw her looking up at him. She nodded her head as if telling him to do what Reverend Johnes asked. Jimmy stood, walked over to the stairs and began his trip to the front of the church. His legs felt like mush and he thought he was going to fall in front of all the people. When he reached the front, Reverend Johnes put his hands on Jimmy's shoulders and whispered to him, "Be brave, Jimmy. I know you're scared but this is another challenge. Face it. In his letter General Washington told me to do this to you. Just tell the people what you saw."

Jimmy turned and faced the congregation. He wasn't sure he could talk and, when he opened his mouth to say something, a squeak came out. He could hear some of the boys in the balcony laugh, but the people in front of him were looking straight at him. They wanted to hear what he had to say.

Finally Jimmy began, "I went to Valley Forge with Mr. Elijah Freeman's wagon train. We had seventeen wagons filled with the supplies you and the others gave for the soldiers." As he talked, the fear began to go away and, as he looked out at the people, he could tell they were interested. "We arrived at Valley Forge in the morning and, when Mr. Freeman learned where the supplies were to be delivered, we went there and began to unload the wagons. I don't know how many soldiers were there. I couldn't see the whole camp, but the soldiers I did see looked very sick and worn down. They told me that other wagon trains from other places were coming in and finally they were getting the food and clothing they needed. I did get to talk with

General Washington and he told me to tell you that when spring comes he hopes once again to bring the war to the British. He didn't know where that would be, but asked that you be ready to give all the help you can. He did look very tired and worried. I don't know what else I can tell you except that the General was very grateful for all your help so far."

Jimmy turned and looked back at Reverend Johnes wondering if what he said was enough.

Reverend Johnes nodded his head at Jimmy and said, "Thank you, Jimmy. You may return to your seat." Looking at the congregation Reverend Johnes continued with his sermon. When the services were completed he walked down the aisle and out the church door, waiting to greet the people as they came out.

As Jimmy emerged from the church, after all the adults had exited, Reverend Johnes nodded to him and signaled that he wanted to speak to him. Jimmy found his grandmother and told her that Reverend Johnes wanted to see him and that he would be home as soon as he could. He waited by the old oak tree that grew in front of the church. His grandfather told him the tree was there when he was a boy. Soon the congregation moved on and Reverend Johnes came over to him.

"Jimmy, Colonel Hathaway came to see me this morning before services. There is another wagon train ready to bring more supplies to Valley Forge. Elijah Freeman is sick and Colonel Hathaway wanted me to ask if you would be the guide for the wagon train. He said you knew the way and knew the ferryman at Easton."

"I'd leave right now Reverend but I have to ask my Ma and Pa and my Grandma first. I'm sure if you would ask them they would say 'yes' right away. Grandma Stiles hasn't left for home yet. She is over there talking to Mrs. Aber."

"I'll go over and talk with her, Jimmy. Wait here."

Reverend Johnes walked over to where Mrs. Aber and Mrs. Stiles were talking. "Excuse me ladies," he said. "May I speak to you just a minute, Mrs. Stiles?"

Jimmy couldn't hear what Reverend Johnes said to his grandmother but he saw her nod her ahead in agreement. Reverend Johnes came back to Jimmy and said, "Your grandmother said you could go and also said she would tell your mother and father where you were. The wagon train is leaving in the morning. Before you go I will give you a letter to General Washington to deliver. Once again, Jimmy, another challenge is facing you."

Chapter Twelve

The Return to Valley Forge

Winter and Spring 1778

The trip to Valley Forge took longer than the first one. It rained almost every day and took longer to cross the Delaware River because of the fast moving current. The roads were muddy and the wagons were forced to go off the road many times to avoid getting stuck in the mire.

On March 9, 1778 Jimmy finally reached the American winter camp at Valley Forge. As on the first trip, the wagon train stopped at the headquarters and Jimmy entered. General Greene was in the front room speaking to several men. He saw Jimmy and motioned for him to wait. When he finished talking to the men General Greene approached Jimmy, "You've returned, Jimmy. What brings you back?"

"We've returned with more supplies, General. Should I deliver them to the same place?"

"No. I'll send one of the soldiers to show the wagoners. It is a different place from where you delivered them the last time. If you will wait in the next room for a minute, I want to ask you something."

"Yes, Sir," said Jimmy.

In a few minutes a soldier came into the room and called to Jimmy, "The General will see you now."

General Greene was standing by a window speaking with two men. Turning around when Jimmy entered, the General said, "Jimmy, here's an old friend of yours."

Jimmy instantly recognized Colonel Daniel Morgan. "Hello, Colonel," he said.

"Hello, Jimmy. It's only been a year since I saw you last and you seem to have grown faster than a garden weed. Jimmy, I want you to meet General Arnold. Benedict Arnold. He is an old friend of mine. We served together at Quebec and Saratoga. When General Greene told me you were here I told General Arnold about your bravery at that action in Springfield and how General Washington was so impressed with your spunk."

Jimmy responded, "Hello, General Arnold. I'm very happy to meet you especially since you are a friend of Colonel Morgan."

"I'm pleased to meet a brave young soldier, Jimmy." said General Arnold, "We are going to need many more of them before this war is over."

General Greene asked, "Jimmy, do you know how to write?"

"Yes, General, my mother, Grandmother Stiles and Reverend Johnes have been teaching me. I'm getting to be quite good at it."

"Good," said General Green. "I have a very important job for you. Do you have to return to Morristown right away?"

"The wagon train is returning tomorrow, General."

The General answered, "What I have in mind will take longer than that. Can you stay in Valley Forge for a week or more?"

"I don't know how I would get home if I missed the wagon train. My mother and grandmother are expecting me to return with it. They would be worried if I didn't."

General Greene asked, "Do you think it would help if I wrote a note to Colonel Hathaway and Reverend Johnes explaining what you are doing?"

"I know it would. They trust both men with anything. The whole town does," answered Jimmy.

"Then, that's what I'll do right now. I'll even have General Washington sign it with me. Wait just a minute, Jimmy, and I'll have that note for you to give to the people on the wagon train to take back to Morristown," said General Greene as he left the room to go into the next office.

Very soon he returned. General Washington was with him.

"Hello, Jimmy," said General Washington, "I see you've met Colonel Morgan and General Arnold. You must like it here in Valley Forge to come back so soon."

"Hello, General Washington. I arrived this morning with another wagon train of supplies from the people of Morristown."

"I signed that note with General Greene. It is addressed to Colonel Hathaway, Reverend Johnes, your Mother and Father, and to your Grandmother. I hope they will understand why we want you to remain here. Come into the next room with me and sit down while I tell you what I want you to do."

Jimmy followed General Washington and sat where the General motioned for him to sit. "Jimmy," the General began, "do you remember the last time you were here I was speaking to Baron von Steuben?"

"Yes, General, when you introduced Mr. Freeman and me to him he never said a word to us. I thought he looked mad."

"He wasn't mad, Jimmy. He didn't understand a word I said to him when I introduced you. He just arrived from Europe and doesn't speak any English. Baron von Steuben is a Prussian. He is an expert in military training and I am using him to train our soldiers but it is very difficult because he doesn't speak English. There is a young boy with him. He's French but speaks both German and English and he serves as the Baron's translator. The boy is seventeen—just a few years older than you. He speaks English English, not American English. That's why I think you can help us. I don't remember the boy's name, but General Greene knows him. I want you to go with General Greene. He will show you what I want you to do."

"Yes. Sir. Thank you for writing that note for me."

Jimmy left and in the next room General Greene led him to a young soldier waiting in the hallway.

"Jimmy, this is Private Jameson. He is going to take you over to the parade ground where Baron von Steuben and his interpreter, Peter Duponceau, are working. I've spoken to Peter and explained to him what I wanted. If you tell him that General Greene sent you he will know what to do with you."

"What is it you want me to do, General?" asked Jimmy.

"Jimmy, Baron von Steuben is training a group of men in military drill and operations. These men have been carefully chosen. Once Baron von Steuben trains them they will become the trainers of the rest of the soldiers here at Valley Forge. With luck, by late May we will have a trained army ready to fight the British. Your job is simple but very important. These trainers are going to need a manual or a guide to teach the other soldiers. Von Steuben doesn't speak English so what he is teaching must be translated from German into English and then written down in English for the manual. Peter will do the translation and Colonel Hamilton will write Peter's English English into American English--

the language American soldiers will understand. Colonel Hamilton will also add the military terms needed since Peter has no experience with military terms. You'll see what I mean about English English when you meet Peter Duponceau and talk to him. Your job, Jimmy, will be to make copies of Colonel Hamilton's translations. We have no printing equipment here at Valley Forge. The nearest printers are in Philadelphia and the British are there. So these manuals will have to be written in longhand. The work will be boring and tedious but it has to be done. Private Jameson, here, will work with you."

Turning to Private Jameson General Greene said, "Private, take Jimmy to the parade ground and introduce him to Peter."

"Yes sir," said Private Jameson and led Jimmy out of the headquarters. Private Jameson, Jimmy learned, was from a Pennsylvania regiment. His name was Aaron and he was sixteen years old. His home was in Lancaster, about fifty miles away, and he had been in the army only a few months. The walk to the parade grounds took about half an hour and along the way Jimmy and Aaron talked about the conditions at Valley Forge and what Baron von Steuben was doing. Aaron told him that the

Baron was a very stern man and that he was a little afraid of him because he shouted and cursed so much at everybody. At the edge of the parade ground Jimmy could see a man shouting orders to a group of about fifteen men. Standing next to him was a young man. Jimmy assumed this was Peter Duponceau.

Aaron and Jimmy watched Baron von Steuben drilling the group of men for awhile. The Baron would shout, Peter Duponceau would shout the translation, and the men would react. It was funny to watch but it was effective. The men were learning. When the drill was ended Aaron and Jimmy walked over to Peter. Aaron introduced Jimmy and Peter knew right away why Jimmy was there.

"Bonjour, Jimmy. You're going to be one of the writers, aren't you?"

"Yes, Peter." Jimmy noticed the different accent and knew he would have to listen intently to understand Peter.

The three boys began to walk slowly back to the headquarters. Peter knew Jimmy was having a hard time understanding what he was saying and spoke slowly. He explained the problem facing the American army. The soldiers were severely undertrained and undisciplined, besides being in very poor health. They were in no condition to meet the best of the British army. Baron von Steuben was working very hard training the specially selected group of soldiers. He was a hard teacher but the soldiers willingly took his shouting and cursing. They knew what he was teaching them could very well save their lives when they met up with the Redcoats and the Hessians. None of them wanted to experience any more defeats like Brandywine and Germantown.

The manuals that Jimmy and Aaron would be making were very important. The work would be tiresome and boring but it would be well worth it if the army could be trained to be ready for the Redcoats and the Hessians.

When they arrived back at the headquarters Aaron and Jimmy were taken to a small room where there was a table and two chairs. They were given quill and ink and told to start copying what Colonel Hamilton had written. Jimmy made copy after copy of the same pages. His hand was sore and he was becoming very bored, but he and Aaron kept going. As fast as they made the necessary number of copies Colonel Hamilton had more pages for them to copy.

Finally, after almost two weeks, they were finished. By writing the manuals many times over Jimmy had learned them by heart. He knew the commands. He knew the drill for loading and firing the muskets. He knew the instructions for using the bayonet. He thought to himself that if it became necessary he could be a good soldier. In fact, he might be a good teacher of soldiers. But that was only a dream.

The original group of soldiers trained by Baron von Steuben—now General von Steuben— were busy training the rest of the soldiers. One day, Jimmy and Aaron walked over to the parade ground. They were amazed to see hundreds of soldiers marching and drilling. The troops now looked like an army. Their health had returned. They marched and drilled smartly. They were in uniforms. You could see they were proud soldiers. It was as if a miracle had occurred.

Several groups of soldiers were being trained in the use of the bayonet. Jimmy remembered copying the instructions on the use of this weapon, but it was much different from reading about its use and actually seeing it put to use. The soldiers were practicing, each with a partner. They would thrust and parry just as the instruction manual taught.

Baron von Steuben had been told that when the Americans met the British and Hessian soldiers armed with bayonets at the battles of Brandywine and Germantown the Americans began to retreat. Von Steuben responded by saying that once a soldier learned how to use a bayonet, the fear of seeing another soldier coming at him with a bayonet would lessen. Jimmy wondered if that were true. He thought back to that day more than a year ago when he was in the front ranks of the Morris Militia at Springfield. He remembered what a frightening sight it was to see those Redcoats and the green-clad Hessians marching toward them with their bayoneted rifles in their hands. Thank goodness they retreated before the militia did.

Chapter Thirteen

The Challenge at Monmouth Court House

June 1778

It was now mid-May. Jimmy had been at Valley Forge for more than two months. He had sent word home several times telling his parents and grandmother that he was well and being kept very busy. In fact, he was enjoying what he was doing. It was better than sweeping up Mr. Arnold's big room. After making the copies of the manuals, he had been doing odd jobs for Colonel Hamilton who made him feel very useful. Aaron was doing the same for General Greene.

In their conversations Aaron had told Jimmy about the awful conditions at Valley Forge. He told of the disease and starvation that the soldiers had to endure. He told Jimmy that Colonel Hamilton had also been very sick. General Washington had sent the Colonel to Albany to tell General Gates to send additional troops to Valley Forge and, while on his trip, he nearly died from some kind of disease. When he returned it took weeks for him to get well.

There were many staff meetings at the headquarters that spring. Jimmy felt like there was something being planned but neither he nor

Aaron knew what it was. A new face had appeared at the headquarters and Jimmy heard him referred to as General Lee. He learned it was General Charles Lee who had been released by the British where he was a prisoner of war. Jimmy realized it was the same General Lee who had been captured that night over a year ago in Basking Ridge—the night he had sent the British soldiers in the wrong direction. Jimmy took an instant dislike, to the man. He was vain and pompous and acted superior to everyone, even to General Washington.

Aaron and Jimmy were kept busy working for General Greene and Colonel Hamilton. When they were not busy they watched the training of the men on the parade grounds and practiced with the bayonet with Peter Duponceau, who was an excellent teacher.

In late May a big drill was planned at the parade grounds. General Washington and his staff were all there. It was quite a show. The changes that had taken place with the army were amazing. Jimmy noticed that the soldiers marched in fours rather than single file as they used to do. He didn't think much about it until Peter Duponceau explained to him that when the soldiers were on a march the length of the line of march was lessened by a factor of four. In other words, a four-mile-long line of soldiers marching single file would be reduced to a mile-long line marching by fours. The army could now cover a distance much faster than before.

In one corner of the parade ground a group of soldiers demonstrated the proper use of the bayonet. Jimmy could see how improved they were and wondered if they ever came upon British troops in a bayonet fight would they be as good as they looked here. At least they had been trained. They wouldn't be like the militia he had been with at Springfield with Colonel Hathaway.

It was now June. Colonel Hamilton had been missing from camp for several days. Jimmy heard that he was sent into New Jersey to keep an eye on the British. All the soldiers at Valley Forge had been ordered to be ready to move at a moment's notice.

When the Colonel returned, General Washington called a special meeting at the headquarters. General Lee, General Greene, General von Steuben, Colonel Hamilton, and Colonel Hamilton's French friend, General Lafayette, attended. The meeting was held in the large room of the headquarters and all those who waited outside wondered what was going on. There were rumors that the British were getting ready to leave Philadelphia and return to New York; that Colonel Hamilton had been on a spy mission to see what the British were doing; that the purpose of the meeting was to plan an attack on the British on their way back to New York.

Jimmy listened and kept his eyes open. The mood at the headquarters was very tense and Jimmy wasn't going to be surprised if things happened quickly.

And they did. On Thursday, June 18 orders were given for the troops to move out. Early in the morning of June 19 the army left Valley Forge, marching four abreast, and headed toward New Jersey.

Colonel Hamilton had gone ahead of the troops. He was to keep an eye on the route of the British army as it marched toward New York. Before he left he instructed Jimmy to stay close to General Washington, make himself useful when he could, stay out of the way when not needed, and be available to do whatever was asked of him. For Jimmy, his instructions couldn't be clearer.

The soldiers and the following wagon trains crossed the Schuylkill River at Swede's

Ford and headed northeast. They passed Crooked Billet Tavern, turned north for Doylestown and then east toward Coryell's Crossing at the Delaware River.

On Tuesday, June 23 the army crossed the Delaware into New Jersey and headed east for Hopewell.

There were no tasks for Jimmy and, following his instructions from Colonel Hamilton, he stayed out of the way riding in a wagon several hundred yards behind General Washington and his staff. The entire American army was staying to the left of the British Army at a distance of about fifteen miles. Jimmy learned from listening to the officers' talk that General Washington planned to attack the rear of the British army but they weren't sure which route the British would take to New York. They could go a more northerly route that would take them to New Brunswick and on to Staten Island or they could head toward Monmouth Court House and on to Sandy Hook. Ahead were soldiers under the command of General Lafayette who were to meet with elements of the New Jersey militia under the command of General Philemon Dickinson.

On Thursday, June 25 the Continental army reached Kingston. Early that morning a soldier approached Jimmy and told him that General Washington had a job for him. He was to report to the General immediately. Jimmy ran forward to the staff area and was told to wait outside the General's tent.

Several minutes later the General summoned him. "Jimmy, I have an important job for you. I want you to accompany Sergeant Troxell to New Brunswick. I am not sure where General Dickinson and the New Jersey Militia are located. I know the general is ahead of the British force but whether he is on their right or left flank I don't know. Sergeant Troxell has a message from me for General Dickinson. I want you to deliver a message to Colonel Hathaway. I'm quite sure Colonel Hathaway and the Morris Militia are just north of New Brunswick but since Sergeant Troxell doesn't know Colonel Hathaway I want you to deliver the message. You will leave immediately. It's about a ten to fifteen mile ride so you should be in New Brunswick shortly after noon. We are now sure that the British are taking the southerly route toward Monmouth Court House and Sandy Hook. You shouldn't run into any Redcoats on your trip. But be careful. Good luck, Jimmy and give Colonel Hathaway my best regards."

"I will, General." responded Jimmy. "I'll return as soon as I can."

"No, Jimmy. I want you to stay with Colonel Hathaway. Within two or three days we are going to attack the British as they move toward New York. You are not a member of any of the units here. You are a member of the Morris Militia and under the command of Colonel Hathaway. I want you to stay with him."

Jimmy was very disappointed with that order. He wanted to stay with the army but an order was an order. He wondered why General Washington was sending him to Colonel Hathaway with orders to stay with him. Whatever the reason, Jimmy had an order that must be obeyed.

The army could only spare one horse so Jimmy had to ride with Sergeant Troxell. Though still early in the morning, the temperature was rising rapidly. The day promised to be very hot and Sergeant Troxell and Jimmy had to be careful not to push their horse too hard. The road was dry and dusty and whenever they came to a stream or pond they stopped briefly to give the horse some water.

Several hours later they arrived at New Brunswick. Sergeant Troxell inquired about the location of General Dickinson's militia. No one knew, but were quite sure the general was not in the New Brunswick area. Jimmy asked where he might find Colonel Hathaway and the Morris Militia forces and was told they were somewhere between the Watchung Mountains and the other side of the Raritan River. Sergeant Troxell told Jimmy he was sorry to have to leave him alone but he had to return to General Washington. Jimmy said goodbye and proceeded on foot to find Colonel Hathaway.

Seeing the Watchung Mountains in the distance Jimmy figured the river was somewhere in-between and started walking. Very soon he saw the river and knew right away he had a problem--how to get across. He was not a good swimmer.

Several hundred feet downstream he saw a man with a flat-bottomed boat getting ready to push it into the water. Jimmy ran over to him and asked, "Are you going to the other side?"

"Yes, young man. Would you like a ride?"

"I sure would," said Jimmy

"Climb in."

Jimmy got in the boat and the man used an oar to push off into the river.

"Where are you going on the other side?"

"I'm trying to find the camp of the Morris Militia," responded Jimmy.

"Well you're in luck. That's where I'm headed, too. I've got some supplies for a Colonel Hathaway. Do you know him?"

"I sure do. I've got a message for him."

"I'll tell you what. I'll take you to him if you help me carry these supplies."

The man rowed steadily and soon reached the opposite bank. Jimmy got out and helped the man pull the boat up on shore.

"The militia camp is about a mile ahead. Not too far. Here, I'll load you up and we'll be off."

The hardest part of the walk was climbing up the river bank which was quite steep. As he approached the militia camp the first man Jimmy recognized was Elijah Freeman. His back was to

Jimmy, but after staring at the back of Mr. Freeman's head during that first trip from Morristown to Valley Forge, Jimmy would recognize Elijah Freeman from any view.

"Hello, Mr. Freeman," Jimmy said as he approached.

Elijah Freeman turned around and saw Jimmy. "Jimmy Stiles! How good to see you. What are you doing here?"

"General Washington sent me to deliver a message to Colonel Hathaway. Is he here?

"Yes, he is, Jimmy. Who is your friend?"

"This is Mr. Henderson. He gave me a ride across the river and has some supplies for Colonel Hathaway."

"Colonel Hathaway is over by that clump of trees. Come with me."

The three walked several hundred feet and Elijah Hathaway called out, "Colonel Hathaway! You have some visitors."

When the Colonel turned and recognized Jimmy he walked toward him saying, "Jimmy Stiles. What brings you here?"

"I have a message for you from General Washington," said Jimmy handing the Colonel the message.

Colonel Hathaway quickly opened the message and read it. Turning to Elijah Freeman he said, "Gather up all the troops, Elijah. I have to speak to them."

Jimmy introduced Mr. Henderson and they left their supplies with a militia member.

Colonel Hathaway asked Henderson what was the quickest way to get the men across the Raritan River.

"There is a bridge up steam about two miles from here at Raritan Landing. That's the quickest way," replied Henderson.

The troops were gathering rapidly and within fifteen minutes Colonel Hathaway spoke to them explaining that they were going to move out at dawn the next day.

Just as the sun began to rise, the militia began its journey. Jimmy rode in Colonel Hathaway's wagon. The Colonel explained as they rode, "General Washington has ordered us to Englishtown where we are to stay put until we're needed. Included in those orders were instructions to take you back in the Morris Militia and to use you in any way I think will help the militia. That is precisely what I am going to do. Do you understand?"

"Yes Colonel," responded Jimmy "I understand."

Colonel Hathaway continued, "Now, Jimmy, tell me what has been going on since I last saw you? We've got a long ride ahead of us, fifteen or twenty miles. We should be near to Englishtown by noon. So, begin your story."

Jimmy told the Colonel about the second trip to Valley Forge and about how bad the conditions were at the winter encampment. He explained his work on the Von Steuben manual and how the training had improved the army. Colonel Hathaway was very interested in that When Jimmy told him he had memorized the manual after making so many copies, he made Jimmy promise he would help train the militia when they all got back to Morristown.

Colonel Hathaway wanted to know about the trip from Valley Forge across New Jersey. Jimmy explained that spies in Philadelphia reported the British were leaving for New York and planned to march across New Jersey rather than return by ship down the Delaware River and up the New Jersey coast. Jimmy told about crossing the Delaware River at Coryell's Crossing on June 23. Once into New Jersey they learned that when the British reached Allentown they took the road to Monmouth Court House and Sandy Hook rather than the road to New Brunswick and Staten Island. The American army was traveling in the same direction as the British but keeping to the left by about fifteen miles. Jimmy told Colonel Hathaway that when General Washington reached Hopewell he called a meeting of his officers and asked for their opinion on what to do. Most of them, including General Lee who was second in charge, wanted to leave the British alone and let them get back to New York. General Washington, however, decided to attack the British before they reached Sandy Hook. Since General Lee disagreed, General Washington put General Lafayette in charge of the attacking army. The next day the Americans reached Kingston and it was there that General Washington sent Jimmy to New Brunswick to deliver the message to Colonel Hathaway.

"What has happened since then, Colonel, I don't know," said Jimmy.

The evening of Friday, June 26 found the men of the Morris Militia encamped in a wooded area on the edge of an open field outside Englishtown. It was a very warm evening and the men were stretched out, sleeping on the ground.

The next morning Colonel Hathaway sent several soldiers into the village of Englishtown to see if there was any sign of the American army. He asked Jimmy to go along with them hoping Jimmy would see some soldiers he knew and get some information from them. He also wanted Jimmy to tell someone in charge where the Morris Militia was located.

As the group reached the edge of the village, it seemed to Jimmy that the whole Continental army was there. There were soldiers everywhere. Suddenly he heard someone shouting, "Jimmy! Jimmy Stiles!" It was Aaron Jameson. The two boys found a place where they could sit down and Jimmy began to ask questions.

"What's happening, Aaron?"

"Jimmy, the last time I saw you was Thursday. So much has happened in the past two days, I don't know where to start. Do you remember General Lafayette was to be in charge of the attacking army? Well, now General Lee is in charge. He must have been mad when General Washington put General Lafayette in charge and asked to be renamed the commander of the attacking force. Just between you and me I think Lafayette was the better choice and so do many of the soldiers. They don't trust Lee as a leader. Anyway, General Lee is here in Englishtown and the attack is being planned for tomorrow morning. The English are about three miles away at Monmouth Court House and General Clinton is letting his soldiers rest today because of the heat. If they continue at the speed they are going they should be at Sandy Hook on Monday. If the attack is not made tomorrow the English will be at the highlands and it will be much harder to attack them there. So it looks like early tomorrow morning Lee will attack."

"Do you know what General Washington has planned for the Morris Militia?" asked Jimmy.

"No. I haven't heard them mentioned. What did General Washington say in his message to Colonel Hathaway?"

Jimmy responded, "He told him to proceed to Englishtown and to wait until he was needed."

"Where is the militia now?"

"We are about a mile from here on the edge of a field."

"It sounds like you should stay there until you hear differently. I'll tell General Greene where you are," said Aaron. "Better yet, you tell him. There he is."

Jimmy approached General Greene who was talking to another officer. Jimmy waited until the General was free and then told him the location of the Morris Militia.

General Greene said, "Tell Colonel Hathaway to stay where he is until we need him. This is going to be a busy day. "

General Greene turned to speak to another man. The general didn't have time for small talk, so Jimmy returned to Aaron.

'Where is General Washington now, Aaron?" asked Jimmy.

'He's somewhere between here and Cranbury with a smaller body of troops. He will move up sometime this afternoon or this evening to be in position to help General Lee."

After spending a few more minutes with Aaron, Jimmy hurried back to report to Colonel Hathaway. He told him everything Aaron had said and reported that General Greene knew where the Morris Militia was located. It was still very hot and the militia soldiers spent the afternoon under the trees at the edge of the field. There was nothing to do but wait. No orders arrived.

That evening Jimmy slept on the ground under a big oak tree. He listened to the many night noises--the various insects and the men snoring. Before dawn Colonel Hathaway woke him and asked him to return to Englishtown to see if he could learn anything more. He ordered Jimmy to report back as soon as he learned anything of importance.

"Jimmy," said Colonel Hathaway, "today you will be my eyes and ears."

Jimmy realized Colonel Hathaway was anxious to be involved in the coming fight. It was difficult for him to sit and wait for the signal to advance.

It was still dark when Jimmy arrived at Englishtown but there was activity everywhere. He found Aaron and asked what was happening.

Aaron told him many of the soldiers had already left for Monmouth Court House and that the attack would probably begin by mid-morning. Aaron knew Jimmy wanted to know what General Greene expected from the Morris Militia and reported to Jimmy that the General told him to tell Jimmy that he knew where Colonel Hathaway's soldiers were located and, if needed, a messenger would be sent to inform the Colonel. Meanwhile they were to wait patiently.

By now the sun had risen and Jimmy could see well enough to run back to the militia encampment. He reported to Colonel Hathaway what was happening and could tell he was disappointed not to be included in the attack. It was very hard to wait while an attack was being readied.

Later that morning the sound of distant cannon could be heard and the men of the militia knew the attack was beginning. For the rest of the afternoon the sounds of war echoed through the air, but no orders arrived.

Late in the afternoon the restless Colonel Hathaway sent Jimmy back to Englishtown to get any news.

In the village there were men gathered in clusters all talking excitedly. Jimmy didn't recognize anyone and moved near one of the groups. He learned the attack began about ten that morning. One man seemed to do all the talking and seemed to know more than the others. Jimmy listened to him carefully.

"The attack began about ten this morning," he said, "We were attacking the rear guard of the British as they marched toward Sandy Hook and the ships to take them to New York. In the beginning it went well. We had them on the run but then the British troops turned and fought back. All of a sudden our soldiers began running to the rear. I couldn't imagine why because we seemed to be doing well. I followed them and wondered what General von Steuben would think of us for running so early in the fight. Then I heard it was General Lee who had given the order to retreat, so I retreated with the other men. While going back, we came upon General Washington and Colonel Hamilton. I never saw the General so mad. He hollered at us, rode his horse back and forth in front of us to block our retreat. I think if he could have got his hands on General Lee right then he would have wrung his neck. Well, urged on by the General and Colonel Hamilton, we turned around and moved forward again and quickly ran into the British who were chasing us. A great fight broke out and this time we learned what the bayonet was for. Thank goodness old von Steuben taught us how to use it. He'd 'a been proud of us. We chased the Redcoats away and then more troops came up to relieve us. I don't think I was ever more hot or tired in my life. From what I hear we are still chasing those Redcoats out of Monmouth Court House. I think we beat them good."

Hearing that, Jimmy raced back to tell Colonel Hathaway.

The Colonel gathered the men around him and said, "I guess they're not going to need us. We might as well make supper and then, in the morning, I'll go into Englishtown and see what we're supposed to do."

That night Jimmy lay on the ground. It was still very warm. Before going to sleep he was thinking that General Washington had sent him to find Colonel Hathaway to keep him away from the coming battle.

At dawn Jimmy went with Colonel Hathaway into Englishtown. The Colonel found General Greene, reported to him, and was told that the British were now on their way to Sandy Hook. The army was not going to pursue them. General Greene told the Colonel the Morris Militia was not needed now and could return to Morristown.

Jimmy and the Colonel returned to the soldiers and by mid-morning the militia was on its way back to Morristown.

Chapter Fourteen

The Homecoming

Summer 1778

Colonel Benoni Hathaway and the Morris Militia began their trip home late in the afternoon of June 30. From Englishtown they stayed south of the Raritan River until it was fordable. Once across the river they stayed to the left of the Watchung Mountains until they reached the flatlands with direct access to Morristown over the Vealtown Road.

Four miles from Morristown Jimmy left the group and turned into the lane that led to home. It was near sundown and he saw his mother in the garden on her knees weeding. She did not see her son coming. Very quietly he approached, knelt down beside her and began to help his mother with the weeding. Her mind must have been far, far away. She did not notice him. As she reached for another weed he put his hand on her hand. Startled, she turned, saw her son and cried, "Jimmy, you're home."

Jimmy's mother held him in her arms. She struggled up on her feet, took his hand and, after a few moments, said, "Come, let's find Pa and your brothers. They're in the barn milking."

As Jimmy and his mother entered the barn they saw Joseph Stiles sitting on a stool with his head resting against the side of a cow. He was busy milking and did not see his wife and son standing there watching him.

"Hello, Pa," said Jimmy.

Jimmy's father turned his head, saw Jimmy, and jumped up so fast that he spilled the milk bucket.

"George! John! Joseph! Boys, come here quick. Your baby brother is home."

Joseph Stiles rushed to Jimmy and picked his son up. The three brothers came around the corner of the barn and they too ran to Jimmy. It was a family reunion similar to the one when Jimmy came home after the pox .

That evening Mrs. Stiles prepared a chicken dinner. Jimmy hadn't eaten so well since he left home almost five months before.

On Saturday the family got into the wagon and traveled to Morristown. There was going to be an Independence Day celebration on the Green and everybody in the area was going to be there.

Chapter Fifteen

Teaching the Militia

Summer and Fall 1778

When the Stiles' wagon reached the Morristown Green a crowd had already gathered for the Independence Day celebration. The boys joined the crowd while their parents went on to Grandma Stiles' house where they left the wagon and let the horses graze out behind the house.

Jimmy walked across the Green to Arnold's Tavern to say hello to Mr. Arnold but also to see if he still had a job. On the way he saw Reverend Johnes, waved to him and went on to the tavern.

Mr. Arnold was waiting at the door, smiling, with a broom in his hand when Jimmy arrived. It appeared he still had his job.

"I'm just fooling you, Jimmy. You don't have to sweep today. Go on over to the Green and enjoy the celebration. It's good to see you home."

"It's good to be home, Mr. Arnold. Thank you for letting me keep my job and thank you for letting me join the celebration."

Jimmy returned to the Green and noticed Colonel Hathaway was there with many members of the Morris Militia. They were preparing to parade around the Green with several drummers and a number of fifers. It was to be a demonstration of their marching skills. Jimmy thought about the march home from Englishtown. If the militia marched here as they did then, the crowd was not going to see much skill.

The parade began and Jimmy stood on the edge of the parade ground with the rest of the crowd. The militia looked like the soldiers marching at Valley Forge before General Von Steuben took over the training. They were not in step; they looked sloppy and undisciplined. When it was over Colonel Hathaway came up to Jimmy and said, "Well, Jimmy, what do you think of the militia?"

Jimmy answered, "I think they need General Von Steuben's training, Colonel."

Colonel Hathaway smiled, "Do you remember when you first met with me outside of New Brunswick and I said I wanted you to help me train the militia when we got back to Morristown? You are already a member of the militia, thanks to Colonel Ford. You have no rank and I can't give you that, but I do want you to show me how to train those men. Can you make me several copies of the training manual you copied at Valley Forge?"

"I know every word. I did it so often it's stuck in my head. How many copies would you need, Colonel?" asked Jimmy.

"I think three or four would do but if you could get several more they certainly would be used."

Just then Jimmy spied Phebe Aber standing with her mother and father at the edge of the Green.

"Excuse me, Colonel. I think I see the way to get those copies to you very fast."

He hadn't seen Phebe since Reverend Johnes asked him to speak to the congregation the past winter. She seemed very happy to see him and Jimmy explained to her what Colonel Hathaway wanted. She was very willing to help; promised she would also get Sarah Mathias to help.

That afternoon the three began their work in a room Mr. Arnold let them use on the second floor of the tavern. Within a few days they had finished the copies and delivered them to Colonel Hathaway.

Colonel Hathaway examined one copy and said to Jimmy, "I don't think I know how to use them. Could you do the training of the men?"

"I don't think so, Colonel," responded Jimmy, "The men won't listen to a young boy. I remember General Von Steuben had to holler at the soldiers quite often and I don't think the militia would take that from me. I could train you and several of your officers, though. I think the men would listen to you and them much better than to me."

"Good idea, Jimmy. When can we start?"

"How about tomorrow? If you ask Mr. Arnold I'm sure he will give me some time off in the morning. We can do what we have to do right behind the tavern on that flat piece back there. Then nobody will see what we're doing."

"I'll go talk to Jake right now and see you tomorrow morning at nine."

The next morning Colonel Hathaway, Elijah Freeman, Caleb Cutler, and John Primrose met behind Arnold's Tavern for school with Jimmy Stiles the teacher. Just before they began, Jacob Arnold came out of the back door of the tavern and asked if he could join the group. Mr. Arnold was a member of the mounted militia but felt he could profit by some of this training. Another onlooker was Reverend Johnes. He was too old to participate but he watched Jimmy proudly as he met this new challenge.

And so they began—five men taking instruction on how to be better soldiers from a fourteen year old boy. It was good they were behind the tavern where they could not be seen for many of the men and women of Morristown might have found this very amusing.

The students learned their lessons well, even the bayonet drills. In a matter of days Jimmy told Colonel Hathaway they were ready to teach the other militia soldiers.

It was no longer necessary to drill behind the tavern, so instruction began on the Green. Every day the militia would drill with their newly trained instructors. At first they looked as untrained as Jimmy remembered the soldiers at Valley Forge were. Slowly improvement came and by the second week of September the Morris Militia looked as well as did those soldiers who took on the British at Monmouth Court House. The drills became an attraction and almost every day near sundown a crowd would gather on the Green to watch. Bayonet practice was the favorite of both the spectators and the trainees.

The men would pair off and with their partners go through the motions of the use of the bayonet. Those who became very good became the instructors of those who were not. In time the Morris Militia were as good, if not better, with the bayonet than the Redcoats or Hessians.

The first snow fall of the winter of 1778-79 had come to Morristown. Business at the tavern was slow and Jimmy was busy cleaning the tables. He listened to several of the customers talking and learned that the army had taken up winter quarters at Middlebrook about twenty miles from Morristown on the road to New Brunswick. It was a safe camp, nestled up against the Watchung Mountains. From the overheard conversations Jimmy learned that the war had moved south, as far south as the Carolinas. The British were still in New York but activity in New Jersey seemed to have stopped. It was very, very quiet in Morristown and Jimmy was very, very bored. He was tired of sweeping floors and waiting on customers at Mr. Arnold's tavern. He longed to be with the army but Reverend Johnes talked some sense into him.

"Why would you want to go to Middlebrook to sit in a hut doing nothing? That's what the army is doing. Don't you think you would be bored there as well?

"I guess so, Reverend."

"I think you should stay here, help your Grandmother through the winter and continue your school work with me. You're better off here than you would be in Middlebrook."

And so Jimmy remained bored in Morristown. The winter of 1778-79 passed slowly with very little snow, very mild temperatures and nothing out of the ordinary to do. The spring and summer of 1779 also passed quietly. Jimmy worked at the tavern, helped Grandma Stiles and spent time with Reverend Johnes talking about the books he had read.

Chapter Sixteen

General Greene Seeks Jimmy's Help

The Fall of 1779

By October, Morristown was in the midst of a serious drought. It hadn't rained since early August and there was very little rain before then. The farmers complained that their crops were poor. The hay in the fields was brittle and as Jimmy walked across the Green he could hear the grass crackle under his feet. He heard men in the tavern talking about another mild winter. Jimmy thought to himself that they didn't know what they were talking about. Grandpa Stiles knew more about weather than all those men put together. He had told Jimmy to watch for two things if you want to predict what a coming winter was going to be like: squirrels and wooley bears.

Squirrels become very active—much more than usual. It's as if they are in a frenzy to gather food for the winter. There were two big oak trees on the edge of the Green. That morning Jimmy noticed a flock of squirrels darting hither and yon about the two trees, gathering acorns. According to Grandpa Stiles that was one sure sign of a bad winter on the horizon. The other was the wooley bears; those fuzzy caterpillars you see in the fall. Wooley bears are about an inch or so long. They are black and brown and look very furry. Grandpa said that if the brown stripe around the wooley bear is narrow that is another sure sign of a bad winter. That morning Jimmy picked up a wooley bear from the Green. It rolled into a ball as they usually do when you touch them. When Jimmy uncurled the caterpillar he saw that the brown stripe was very narrow.

Those men in the tavern didn't know what they were talking about. Jimmy wondered if they ever watched the squirrels or looked at wooley bears. Of course, they weren't as smart as Grandpa was. Jimmy also knew that Grandpa was telling him to gather extra firewood for Grandma. She was going to need it for sure.

It was early November and Morristown already had its first snowfall—about two inches. Jimmy was cleaning the snow off the tavern's porch when Mr. Arnold came to the door and asked him to come inside. Jimmy went into the big room and saw General Greene. He hadn't seen the General since he was in Englishtown during the Monmouth battle.

The General turned and saw Jimmy. "Jimmy Stiles, how good to see you again. Mr.

The Harder The Conflict

Arnold, do you have a room where Jimmy and I can talk?"

"Yes, Sir. Follow me, please."

Mr. Arnold led them to a room down the hallway off the big room.

"This is available, General."

The room had a table and several chairs with a window that looked out on the rear of the tavern. The General asked Jimmy to sit down and then said, "General Washington has sent me on a special mission to Morristown and asked me specifically to speak to you for three reasons. One, he said, and these are his words, 'Jimmy Stiles is not a blatherskite.' Do you know what a blatherskite is, Jimmy?"

"No sir, I never heard that word before."

"Blatherskite," continued General Greene, "is a Scotsman's word for a person who talks too much. I agree with the General. I know you can keep a secret because you have many times since I've known you. Jimmy, the secret this time is that General Washington is bringing the army back to Morristown for the winter encampment. He has sent me to find a suitable place for the troops. That brings me to the other two reasons he wanted me to speak to you. The General said you knew this area as well as anyone. The third reason is that he believed no one would become suspicious seeing me talking to a boy. We can't afford to have the British find out that the Continental army is moving into the area. The army on the move is very vulnerable to a British attack and the General wants the army safe and secure in Morristown before the British find out about the move. Do you understand why this must be a secret for awhile?"

"Yes, sir," answered Jimmy. "I'm not a blatherskite."

"Good," replied General Greene. "Now, here is what I'm looking for. I would like the camp to be located away from the center of the town so the townspeople will not have the problem of six or seven thousand soldiers trying to live within a town of two to three hundred people. I want the camp to be near an abundant source of wood for the making of huts and for firewood. I don't want the camp located in a flat area like Valley Forge was. That was the cause of so much of the sickness there. There was no place for proper drainage. I want the camp to be located in a hilly area so that rain and waste will not wash into the huts. Can you find such a place, Jimmy?"

Jimmy sat quiet for a minute or so thinking. Then he said, "I think I know of such a place, General. It is very near my father's farm. I know it very well because I've hunted and trapped in the area many times. For what you've described I think it would be just right. There are many springs and small brooks so there is a good water supply, too. Do you want me to show you?"

"How far away is this place, Jimmy?"

"About four miles."

"It's late afternoon. I want to see it but I want enough time to look around. It will be dark soon. Why don't we ride out early tomorrow morning? Is that all right with you?" asked General Greene.

"I can go anytime you want if it's all right with Mr. Arnold."

I'll speak to him right now."

General Greene left the room and moments later returned. He said, "Mr. Arnold gave his permission and said to take as much time as we needed. I'll meet you here early tomorrow morning and I will have a horse available for you."

When Jimmy arrived for work the next morning General Greene was waiting in the big room. They quietly left the tavern, mounted their horses and rode off. It began to snow, a very light snow, but enough to cover the road.

As they rode along General Greene said that he hoped this winter would be as mild as the last one. Jimmy told him about his grandfather's weather signs and mentioned the squirrels and the wooley bear he saw on the Green. The General replied, "Oh, I hope you're wrong. I'm not sure the army could take another winter like the one we had at Valley Forge."

Ten minutes later they came to the road to Mendham.

"We turn right here, General. My father's farm is just ahead and to the left. This land and big house to the right is Mr. Kemble's. I think you remember him from the last time you were here. He is known to be a Tory but nobody pays much attention to him because he's so old. I find him to be a nice old man and I don't think he will be any trouble. I don't know who owns the land I'm going to show you but I suspect it's either

151

Mr. Kemble or Mr. Henry Wick, or both. Mr. Wick has a farm about a mile and a half farther on this road."

A few hundred yards in on the road to Mendham Jimmy pointed out a large house to the right.

"That's Mr. Kemble's home. We are going to turn off on to a trail to the right a little further ahead."

The snowfall had increased and Jimmy pulled the collar of his coat up around his neck. They turned on to the trail and rode silently for several minutes. They were in a thick forest. General Greene dismounted and walked into the woods. A few minutes later he returned.

"These are mostly oak, walnut and chestnut trees, Jimmy. This will be good for the construction of huts and firewood, but it's a little too flat for what I want."

"In just a few minutes we will reach the area where the ground rises. I think you will find that better," responded Jimmy.

Ahead they could see the beginning of a tree-covered hill. As their horses climbed the hill General Greene's face showed that he was beginning to like the area. Off to one side was a ravine with a small brook running through it. They rode further for a few minutes and suddenly General Greene stopped and turned to Jimmy.

"This is far enough. You picked a good spot. The hills here are fine. They are steep enough for drainage and there is good protection. This will be the location of the encampment. Let's go back to Morristown."

The snow continued and by the time they got back to the tavern there was already several inches on the ground.

Before they entered the tavern General Greene told Jimmy, "I'm leaving right away for Newburgh where General Washington is. In several days I will send a work party here of several hundred men. They will be led by Major Dawson. I want you to meet him at the tavern. The men will stay out of sight outside of town. I don't want any signal that this is going to be the winter encampment until the main army gets here. Your job is to lead Major Dawson and his men to Jockey Hollow and leave. They will begin work on the camp. Do you understand?"

"Yes, sir."

"I'll be leaving now. Thank you, Jimmy. Once again you have proven to be worth your weight in gold."

A week later a Major Dawson arrived at Arnold's Tavern and asked where he could find Jimmy Stiles. Several townspeople saw the major and Jimmy riding out on the Vealtown Road but thought nothing of it.

Chapter Seventeen

The Continental Army Returns to Morristown

Winter 1779

Since Major Dawson's arrival in Morristown there had been two more snowfalls. On November 30 a third storm occurred, this time bringing nine more inches of snow. The snow continued into the next day--the day that General George Washington and the Continental Army returned to Morristown.

Jimmy was once again sweeping and shoveling snow off the porch that extended across the front of Arnold's Tavern. He had been watching the soldiers slowly walking past and wondered how they could keep going. They looked so tired and so woebegone. He noticed that some had no shoes but had wrapped rags around their feet. Colonel Hathaway came up on the porch and told Jimmy that these soldiers had been walking for six days. Newburgh, New York, their former camp was one hundred and twenty miles away. Though they cursed the snow they nevertheless realized the snow had protected them from British attack during their trip. Jimmy was thinking how pathetic the poor men looked when one soldier caught his eye. He knew this man from some place. He looked more intently and then rushed off the porch to the man.

"Aaron! Aaron!," he shouted. It was his friend from Valley Forge—Aaron Jameson, the young soldier from Pennsylvania. Aaron looked strangely at him with a blank look that told Jimmy there was something very wrong with Aaron. Jimmy called to Colonel Hathaway for help and he ran to Jimmy's side.

"Colonel, would you help me with this soldier. He's my friend and he looks like he's about to die."

When they reached for Aaron he began to holler saying he could not stop or they would shoot him for deserting. The colonel and Jimmy carried the struggling soldier off the street and into the big room of the tavern. Aaron was delirious. They took him into one of the back rooms and put him on a bunk. With that Aaron passed out and all the fight went out of him. Colonel Hathaway told Jimmy to get the wet clothes off Aaron. It was then that Jimmy saw that Aaron had no shoes. He had rags wrapped around his feet and tied with a strip of cloth. When Jimmy removed the frozen rags he saw that Aaron's feet were blue. He asked Colonel Hathaway to look at them.

"He's got frostbite," said the Colonel. "His hands are frostbitten, too, Jimmy. We've got to warm him up but we have to go slow. Going too fast is almost as bad as the frostbite. He might lose the feet and hands. Get the rest of those clothes off and then get some blankets on him. I'll get some tea and you see if he will sip it slowly."

Colonel Hathaway left the room to get the tea and Jimmy went to find some blankets. When Jimmy returned, Aaron had come to and asked where he was. Jimmy told him and asked if he knew who he was. Aaron didn't recognize Jimmy and appeared afraid. Jimmy said to him, "Aaron, this is Jimmy Stiles. Do you remember me? We worked together copying General Von Steuben's drill manual at Valley Forge. I saw you again at Englishtown a year ago. Don't you remember me?"

Aaron looked puzzled and at last he smiled and said,

"Jimmy. Jimmy Stiles."

'It's me, Aaron. You're safe. You're in Morristown, Aaron. This is where I live."

Suddenly Aaron became frantic again and cried out, "Jimmy! Help me, Jimmy. I'm a deserter. I've left my brigade. They will shoot me when they catch me."

Just then Colonel Hathaway returned with the tea and heard Aaron's cry.

"Don't worry, boy," said the Colonel, "I know your commanding officer, Colonel Hand. I will take care of this. You haven't deserted but you need care or you're going to die. Now calm down."

Turning to Jimmy he then said, "Listen to that cough and that rattle in his chest. I'm afraid this boy has lung fever. I'm going over to the church and get Doctor Campfield to look at him. I saw him talking to Reverend Johnes just before I came here."

Jimmy held the mug of tea to Aaron's lips while he sipped. The mug was almost empty when Colonel Hathaway returned with Doctor Campfield. The doctor took a close look at Aaron, put his ear to Aaron's chest and said, "This soldier has lung fever all right. Jimmy, take this boy to Grandma Stiles. She will know what to do with him. Tell her I sent him."

Mr. Arnold, who was watching what was happening, said, "Jimmy, get Dolly, hitch her to the wagon and bring it around to the front of the tavern. I'll get some men to carry the boy out and you take him to your Grandma's."

"Yes sir," said Jimmy.

Aaron was loaded into the back of the wagon. One of the men, Uriah Johnson, who lived near Grandma Stiles, went with Jimmy to help him get Aaron into Grandma's house.

The wagon pulled up to the front of Grandma's house and they carried Aaron inside. They put Aaron into a bunk just off the kitchen. The temperature outside was below freezing but Grandma's fireplace kept the house warm. She looked at Aaron and seemed to know just what to do.

Jimmy watched. He knew he was watching an expert at work. Dr. Campfield used Grandma Stiles to take care of many of his patients. It seemed that the whole town felt Grandma knew almost as much about curing people as Dr. Campfield did.

She took a container from a shelf and poured out what looked like yellow seeds. She told Jimmy to use the round stone to grind the seeds into a powder.

'What is this, Grandma?" Jimmy asked.

"It is mustard seed," said Grandma. "We're going to make a paste and spread it on Aaron's chest. Sounds funny, but it works. I've seen your Grandpa use it on horses and cows that had lung fever and most of the time it worked on them, too."

She poured hot water into the ground mustard seed and stirred until it was a paste. She then spread it on a rag and wrapped it around Aaron's chest.

"Now, Jimmy, your job is to change that paste every time it gets cool. We've got to keep that chest warm. There's something in that mustard seed that pulls out all the bad things making Aaron sick."

Those mustard seeds must have worked because after a few days Aaron's cough went away. There were no more rattles in his chest. His blue feet and hands turned to normal color and he didn't lose them. Grandma said that most of the time just keeping a sick person warm will cure the frostbite. It's worse when you try to rush a cure.

While he was getting well, Aaron told Jimmy about his trip from Newburgh. Just before they left a snowstorm came. They had no warm clothing. The trip to Morristown took six days and another storm came the day before they arrived. Aaron said he lost his shoes the fourth day and wrapped his feet in rags.

Jimmy said, "You were so bad off when I first saw you I don't think you would have lasted the day. You had three or four more miles to walk and when you reached the camp site there was no shelter. You didn't have a tent and no huts were built yet. You would have had to sleep on the ground that was covered with almost two feet of snow. You wouldn't have lasted the night, Aaron."

"I have to get back to my unit, Jimmy. I'm going to get in trouble."

"No you're not," said Jimmy, "I saw Colonel Hathaway yesterday and he said he talked with Colonel Hand. You are now assigned to General Greene like you were in Valley Forge. I am, too. We can work together. I think learning how to read and write helped us both. General Greene has been made the Quartermaster General and is now responsible for making sure the soldiers have enough to eat and proper shelter to keep them out of the cold. Much of the food is going to have to come from local farmers and, since I know the area and the people in the area,

General Greene wants me to help his staff gather in the necessary food and equipment. I asked him if you could work with me. He remembered what a good job you did with the training manual at Valley Forge and agreed to add you to his staff."

On December 9 a two-day snow storm struck. Morristown shut down. There was hardly any movement in the town. The wind howled and the snow seemed to come down in horizontal waves. Grandma, Jimmy and Aaron stayed inside as did almost everyone else in Morristown. Jimmy thought about the soldiers in Jockey Hollow. They didn't have enough time to build huts for all of them. Many of those poor men must have to sleep in the snow. Jimmy could hear the wind-driven snow beating against the house and was glad he could get close to the fireplace.

When the storm ended Jimmy put on his boots and heavy coat, saddled Prince, Grandma's horse, and rode to the tavern. He was still working for Mr. Arnold in addition to doing the jobs General Greene had for him. He shoveled the snow away from the entrance to the tavern and cleared off the porch. Then he walked across the Green to General Greene's office. It was in the same place as the last time he was in Morristown.

General Greene was getting ready to go on an inspection trip to Jockey Hollow to see how the soldiers had weathered the storm. He asked Jimmy to ride along with him. Jimmy ran back to the tavern, got Prince, and caught up with the General's group as they rode out on the other road to Jockey Hollow. This road ran parallel to the Vealtown Road, but was a shorter route to the campsite. As they rode Jimmy listened to the General describe how his staff had planned the site. The huts would all be the same size: fourteen feet wide, sixteen feet long, and six feet in height at the eaves. Inside would be a small fireplace and bunks for twelve men. It would be a tight fit but it would get the men through the winter. The huts were to be built on the sides of hills for proper drainage and where possible, the huts would face the southern side of the hill to get as much heat from the sun as possible.

Jimmy had heard that there might be as many as eight thousand soldiers in Jockey Hollow and quickly figured there would be almost eight hundred huts. That would be almost like a city.

As they approached the site they could hear the noise of construction as axes and saws were in use. When Jimmy saw the campsite he was awestruck. It seemed that only a short while ago he rode here with General Greene. It was a hillside covered with trees. Now the trees had been cut down; many huts were already built and there were soldiers everywhere, all busy building more huts.

General Greene dismounted and inspected many of the huts. He talked to the men and seemed satisfied with what had been done so far. There were still many soldiers who had no hut to sleep in and there was no reason to tell them to get busy. They were busy because their survival depended on it. The major complaint the soldiers had was the shortage of tools—axes, saws, shovels, and picks. General Greene promised them he would do what he had to do to get these tools to them. When they returned to Morristown he called a meeting of his staff and the leaders of the Morris Militia and informed them that he needed tools and food. They were instructed to ask for donations first. If that proved to be not enough, they were to take what they needed and keep a record of what had been taken. General Greene explained that he had every intention to pay back anything that was taken from the people and added that though he hated to use such methods he had to keep the soldiers from freezing and starving to death.

After the meeting, he told Jimmy to go with the militia men, to keep his own list of what was taken from the people and report to him the reaction of the people. General Greene knew if he didn't have the support of the people in the area all was lost.

On December 15 another two-day snow storm arrived closing all roads and preventing needed food supplies from reaching the troops at Jockey Hollow. The militia and the people in the area joined together to open the roads but it was evident that a serious crisis was coming. The food supplies in the area were almost gone. The drought of the past summer had crippled the harvest and the people had hardly enough to feed themselves without having to feed eight thousand additional soldiers. General Greene was beside himself trying to do what had to be done to keep the army intact. Soldiers were dying every day from the cold and sickness brought on by inadequate food. Others were quietly walking away from Jockey Hollow and going home, wherever home was.

Conditions at Jockey Hollow for the Christmas of 1779 were horrible. Though hundreds of huts had been built there were still men living without shelter. Many had no food. The times were desperate and Jimmy thought to himself that this made Valley Forge look easy.

Jimmy hadn't been home in weeks and now it was almost impossible to travel the Vealtown Road to his father's farm. He was lucky to have Grandma Stiles' house nearby. Aaron was living there with them and his health had returned to normal. Grandma Stiles had saved Grandpa's clothes and boots and thankfully they fit Aaron. He and Jimmy went every day to General Greene's office to do whatever chores the general had for them. Most of their time was spent on horse-drawn sledges packing down the snow to make passage by sled easier.

On Christmas Day Jimmy hitched Prince to the sleigh and took Grandma and Aaron to church. Despite the deep snow there were many people there. Reverend Johnes' sermon was an appeal to the people to do what they could to help the army. Reverend Johnes knew the success of the war depended on what would happen in Morristown in the coming days.

Chapter Eighteen

The Hazardous Trip to Hackettstown

Winter 1780

Two days after New Year's over two feet of snow covered the ground in Morristown. Jimmy was keeping a path cleared to the barn so he could feed the animals. Prince was in his stall covered with a blanket. The chickens were huddled together in their corner and Jimmy gathered nine eggs from their nests. He thought of the chicken dinner Grandma had prepared for Christmas and seemed able to still smell the aroma that filled the house. Climbing into the mow he began to fork hay down into Prince's stall, then went to the other side and did the same into Mable's stall. Mable had to be milked before he went inside because Jimmy felt in his bones that another storm was brewing and he did not want to leave the poor cow overnight without being milked.

He finished his chores in the barn. Mable got an ample supply of corn and Prince, his oats. Before leaving, Jimmy took the two pair of snow shoes hanging on the hook by the barn door. He knew he was going to need them.

Making sure the barn door was closed tightly, Jimmy looked to the grey sky. The pale sun had a circle around it—a sure sign that a storm was coming according to his Grandpa. The wind had picked up and was blowing out of the eastern sky. Aaron came out of the house and the two boys made repeated trips to the woodshed and brought in many logs. "Let the snow come," thought Jimmy, "we're ready."

Just before sundown the flakes appeared. They were very small, very fine—another sign, Grandpa had said, of an impending big storm.

About an hour after supper Aaron, Jimmy and Grandma were sitting by the fire. Grandma was telling stories about when she was a little girl. Jimmy had heard them before but politely listened. Suddenly she stopped and looked to the window.

"The wind is increasing," she announced, "Go look out the door, Jimmy."

Jimmy was lying in front of the fireplace. He got up, opened the door slightly and peered out. The snow wasn't falling; it was blowing straight across. The path to the barn was no more. It had completely filled in. The snow began to blow into the house so he shut the door quickly. There was nothing more that could be done. The animals were fed and safe. The house seemed to be secure and the storm was kept outside where it belonged. They all went to bed.

The next morning the storm continued as fiercely as before. It went on all day and then into the next night. On the second day it gave no sign of stopping. Grandma said she had never seen such a storm in all her days. It finally stopped late on the third night. When Jimmy awoke and looked out, the sun was just peeking over the eastern horizon. Everything looked and sounded so serene. Drifts had formed and covered almost half the window. The snow was up to the eaves on the barn. The fence, that extended from the barn, had disappeared under a white blanket. Jimmy and Aaron put on their heavy coats and boots, forced open the door and trudged to the barn. In some places the drifted snow was over their heads. They returned to the house and put on the snowshoes. Instead of sinking into the snow they were able to walk on top of it. They fed the animals and Jimmy and Aaron took turns milking Mabel. As they were returning to the house they heard the cannon on the Green –the alarm for the militia to meet. Jimmy told Grandma they had been called and the boys, with their snowshoes on, went off to the Green.

Benoni Hathaway was waiting by the porch of the tavern and slowly the militia members gathered around. The men were mumbling to each other wondering what the emergency was. When it appeared that enough men were there Colonel Hathaway began.

"Men, General Greene informed me this morning that starvation is killing many of the soldiers in Jockey Hollow. He said that they have run out of food and can last only a few more days. We have learned that a large supply of food and provisions has reached Hackettstown but can't go any further because of the snow. We have been ordered to open a road to Hackettstown and bring that food to Jockey Hollow as quickly as possible. General Washington said that unless this crisis is met the war is lost. We will need sleighs, of course, but most of all we need sledges—weighted sledges to pack the snow so sleighs can ride over it. My plan is to make a line of sledges and proceed as rapidly as possible to Hackettstown. I'm not familiar with that part of the county but I hear that Hackettstown is about twenty or thirty miles from here. I wish Captain Joseph was still with us. He laid out the path of all these roads and knew the territory like the back of his hand. Elijah Freeman worked with Captain Stiles and is familiar with that area.

Elijah, tell us what you think is the best way to get to Hackettstown in this snow."

Elijah was a big man with hands to match. He spoke very little and when he did he said his words very slowly, deliberately. What he said, people knew to listen and pay heed to.

"We haven't got time to dig our way to Hackettstown," he began, "So we have to pack down this snow tight enough so the runners of the sleighs won't sink into it. I think we should fasten boards together so we have a piece of wood ten feet by ten feet, say, maybe five such pieces— and lay them on the snow, march a team of oxen pulling a sledge on one piece to push the snow down. Just keep picking that piece up and laying another down in front of oxen. Then follow behind the team with several more teams of oxen pulling sledges to pack the snow down further. Then the horse-drawn sleighs can follow. It will be slow-going, but right now I can't think of a better way to do it. As for the route we take—if it were summer I would go to German Valley and over the mountain—but with this snow we'd never get the caravan over the mountain there. It's too steep. So I suggest we go to Suckasunny, to Lake Kaukaunning and then down the hill into Hackettstown. The hills beyond Succasunny are not as steep as the one in German Valley. It will be a little bit longer but, I think, easier."

Not having a better idea the men agreed and the meeting ended. Colonel Hathaway told the group to round up as many sledges, sleighs and boards they could find and be back at the Green as quickly as possible.

By early afternoon they reassembled on the Green. The flat boards were quickly put together and four men were assigned to care for each piece. There were eight sledges and eight teams of oxen. In addition there were twelve sleighs.

Each sledge would carry a load of field stone to pack the snow. There would be a lead sledge pulled by two oxen, followed by another but staying to the right of the lead so as to make the trail wider than the width of a single sledge. This would be followed by another two sledges in the same configuration. The other four sledges would follow and every so often they would alternate the oxen so the oxen leading the group would get some rest. The lead oxen bore the greatest burden as they blazed a path.

Colonel Hathaway sent Aaron to General Greene's office. He said Aaron was not in good enough condition to make the trip. Aaron, very disappointed, followed orders.

The first hour of the journey was somewhat easy if you weren't the lead team of oxen. Then they reached the hill about three miles out of Morristown and the procession slowed considerably. Jimmy thought to himself, "If this is hard, imagine what that hill outside of German Valley would be like--bad enough going up, but treacherous coming down with loaded sleighs and sledges. I'm glad they agreed to Mr. Freeman's suggestion."

By sundown they had reached the section Mr. Freeman called Walnut Grove. They rested and fed the animals. Several hours later they continued on their journey. Colonel Hathaway had sent a rider ahead to alert the residents that the group was coming through. In the morning when they reached Suckasunny they found that farmers had gathered their oxen and sledges to help make the trail and go with them on to Hackettstown. They rested and fed the animals again. Too much depended on the oxen and horses to risk overworking them. Rest now would help insure the success of their task.

The next day they passed Lake Kaukaunning and by nightfall were descending the steep hill into Hackettstown. The men of Hackettstown came to meet them.

The provisions were there as General Greene had said. The residents of Hackettstown had already loaded many sleighs and sledges. The remaining provisions were loaded on the sleighs and sledges from Succasunny and Morristown for the trip back.

As soon as the animals were rested and fed, Colonel Hathaway got the caravan underway. He knew time was precious. The provisions, especially the food, were needed immediately at Jockey Hollow before more died of starvation.

The trip up Hackettstown Mountain was tedious and slow. The caravan followed the path it had already created. When the sledges and sleighs reached the crest everyone stopped and rested before commencing the downhill trek to Lake Kaukaunning. The weather was cold but it was sunny and all were thankful that no snow appeared to be coming. Yet, they all knew that another storm could occur before they returned to Morristown.

The caravan passed Succasunny and decided to try to make the first hill beyond that small village. Reaching the crest Elijah Freeman warned Colonel Hathaway that the oxen needed rest. It was obvious the Colonel was intent on reaching Morristown but Elijah's advice was too valuable to ignore. Colonel Hathaway ordered everyone to stop, feed the animals and rest. By dawn the next morning they were coming into Walnut Grove. At mid-morning Jimmy looked skyward and saw that thin veil of clouds that made the sun dim. He also noticed the tell-tale ring around the sun and wondered if they would make Morristown before the snow began. The end was so close, only a few miles more to go, but a big hill that had to be descended before their mission was complete. By mid-afternoon snowflakes appeared. Within the hour the wind, coming from the northeast, intensified, but the snow had changed to sleet, stinging Jimmy's face as he trudged along.

The caravan was moving slowly up the hill beyond Walnut Grove. It would soon be on the short plateau before descending into Morristown. Jimmy suddenly slipped and fell. He got up quickly and realized there was a thin glaze of ice on top of the snow. A half mile ahead they would begin the walk down the hill. Jimmy wondered if it would be a walk, a slide or a catastrophe.

About a hundred yards before the descent began, Colonel Hathaway stopped the caravan and brought several men to the front.

"Once we go over this crest," he said, "we could be in trouble. There is a coat of ice atop the snow path we made coming up the hill. We must be very careful that no sledge or sleigh gets away on us and starts sliding down the hill. The oxen, the horses and the driver will all be in danger. It is almost a mile to the bottom of the hill and every foot of it will be dangerous. This is my plan. The sledges and sleighs will stay at least a hundred feet apart. There will be one driver on the sledge or sleigh. No one else. I want one man holding the yoke of each ox or the bridle of each horse as we go down the hill. If the animal acts jittery, try to steady it. The front men, the driver and the animals must work together to control the speed and direction of the sledge. When you reach the bottom of the hill, come on back to the top and take another team down. This is going to take time but we've come too far to get careless now. Did I miss anything or do you have anything to add?"

Colonel Hathaway waited for any response. When none came, he said, "Let's go."

Elijah Freeman drove the first sledge. Micah Fairchild steadied the ox on the left, Jimmy, the right, and they began the descent. Jimmy could feel his ox was jittery, unsure of its footing on the icy slope. Jimmy looked at the sledge's shaft that the oxen were attached to and realized the only thing keeping the sledge from sliding down the hill were the oxen. He spoke into his ox's ear trying to calm the frightened animal. It seemed to work as the animal slowly and carefully began the walk down the hill. With every step forward Jimmy watched the sledge hoping it wouldn't start sliding out of control.

The sleet had turned back to snow. Jimmy and all the others were soaked to their skin and now the temperature was dropping. His hands were numb but he held on to the yoke and continued talking to the ox. The mittens he had were frozen and Jimmy wondered if his hands would become frostbitten like Aaron's had been and then knew .at this moment. that was the least of his worries.

When they were at Walnut Grove, Colonel Hathaway had sent a messenger ahead to tell General Greene where they were and to ask if he would send soldiers to help them into town. In the distance, at the foot of the hill, Jimmy could see torches moving toward him. He hoped they were those soldiers.

By now there were four teams of oxen on the hill and many more sleighs to follow. It would be midnight or later before the entire caravan reached the bottom of the hill, that is if they had no runaway sleighs.

The torches came closer and closer. Mr. Freeman hollered and asked them to identify themselves.

A voice was heard, "We're from the Third Brigade, Connecticut Volunteers. We've come to help you."

In the direction of the voice, a face appeared from behind the light of a torch. Elijah Freeman greeted the soldier. "Glad to see you, patriot. We sure do need your help. I'm Elijah Freeman, Sergeant in the Morris Militia. My commanding officer is Colonel Benoni Hathaway. He's somewhere further back up the hill."

"Good evening, Sergeant. I'm Lieutenant Samuelson. I have two hundred men with me ready to help you anyway we can. What do you want us to do?"

Elijah briefly explained what they were doing and asked the Lieutenant if he would move his men up the hill dropping off several men to stay with each sledge or sleigh to help control their descent down the hill. The Lieutenant agreed and moved out.

A half-hour later Jimmy's sledge reached the bottom. Mr. Freeman, Mr. Fairchild and Jimmy could not stop to rest but had to move on to make way for the sledges and sleighs behind them. As dawn came they entered Morristown and were surprised to be greeted by cheers from a crowd that had gathered on the Green. There were many soldiers there who took over the caravan and relieved the militia men. There were fresh animals available to give the poor oxen and horses a well-deserved rest.

Aaron was there with General Greene who told Jimmy to go to his grandmother's house and unfreeze. He said he looked like a snowman.

The soldiers took the provisions to Jockey Hollow and several days later more supplies arrived from Vealtown. General Greene reported to General Washington. "Starvation was prevented, the army survived, thanks to the men of the Morris Militia."

Jimmy went to his Grandmother's who repeated what she had done for Aaron when he arrived a month ago. She even coated him with that hot mustard mush.

In several days he was warmed up and ready for another challenge.

Chapter Nineteen

The Trial—A Judgment of Character

January 1780

Jimmy returned to General Greene's office on the Green two days later completely unfrozen. The General wanted to see his hands and judged them to be fine. No damage done from the frostbite.

"Your grandmother must be quite the healer," he said, "Remind me to go to her if I ever get sick or hurt. Jimmy, things are quiet here right now. Mr. Arnold said if I had nothing for you to do to send you over to the tavern. He could use some help. Aaron is over there right now doing some odd jobs for him."

Jimmy crossed the Green on a path that had been cleared through the three foot deep snow. He wondered if he would ever see green grass or tree leaves again.

His broom awaited him at the tavern and he quickly began sweeping in the big room. He noticed a man sitting at one of the tables reading and as he got closer realized it was General Arnold, the man Colonel Morgan introduced him to at Valley Forge.

"Good morning, General Arnold." said Jimmy.

The General looked up, returned the greeting and added, "Do I know you?

"Sir, we met at Valley Forge. Colonel Morgan introduced us. My name is Jimmy Stiles."

"Oh, yes. I remember. You're the young man Colonel Morgan told me about—staring down the Hessian bayonets in that skirmish at Springfield. What are you doing here sweeping floors?"

'I've worked here for over three years, General."

"But what were you doing in Valley Forge?"

"I was there delivering supplies the people of this area gave to the army and while I was there General Greene asked me to do something for him. So I stayed there and returned to Morristown after the battle at Monmouth. I am a member of the Morris Militia and am attached as an aide to General Green as long as he's here in Morristown. He has nothing for me to do this morning so here I am sweeping Mr. Arnold's floor."

"How old are you?" asked General Arnold.

"I'll be sixteen my next birthday, then I can join the army. My mother and father wouldn't let me before I was sixteen."

"Jimmy, when you do join, I hope you won't be as disappointed as I am right now." General Arnold went back to reading.

Jimmy wondered what he meant by that and asked, "Have you seen Colonel Morgan? I thought he might be here but I haven't seen him."

General Arnold looked up at Jimmy and said, "Colonel Morgan resigned and went home. He lives in Winchester, in Virginia. I resigned once. I should have stayed resigned."

He went back to his reading and Jimmy thought it best not to respond and finished sweeping the floor. Mr. Arnold had Aaron carrying in logs for the fireplaces and Jimmy helped him finish the work. It was now noon and they returned to General Greene's office.

The general was in the front room. When he saw Jimmy he said, "I just returned from

General Washington's headquarters. He was asking about you and wanted to see you. I have some papers here that I want you to take to him. Take Aaron along with you and then both of you go home. I have no more jobs for you today."

It was almost a mile down Morris Street to the Jacob Ford house where General Washington had made his headquarters. Mrs. Ford was Reverend Johnes' daughter and Jimmy had been to the house many times with his grandmother and grandfather. Tim Ford was two years older than Jimmy. Tim was the one who got Jimmy interested in exploring the woods and taught him a lot about the animals in the area. Though Tim was a militia member, Jimmy hadn't seen him in months. He heard that Tim was with a militia group guarding Hobart Gap. He hadn't seen Mrs. Ford since Colonel Ford died. So while he delivered the papers to the general he thought he would pay his respects to Mrs. Ford and ask about Tim.

As they approached the Ford house Jimmy was thinking about the days he spent exploring the Whippanong River looking for beavers. The river was only about a quarter mile behind the house. He wondered if beavers hibernated like bears and if they were as cold sleeping in their dams as he was on that Hackettstown trip.

There were many guards in front of the Ford home. General Greene had given Jimmy a pass for both Aaron and him to enter the home. Jimmy had to show that pass three times before they got to the front door. When they entered they were quickly taken to a side room where General Washington was sitting at a desk. He looked up and smiled.

"Jimmy Stiles. It's good to see you, son."

"Good afternoon, General. General Greene sent me to deliver these papers to you."

General Washington responded, "He sent you because I asked him to send you. The papers are a good excuse. Jimmy, do you remember when I introduced you to Colonel Morgan and told you to watch him and study him carefully?"

"Yes, Sir. You told me your best education came from studying people—especially people you respected. You told me to watch for their strengths and to note their weaknesses. And then you assigned me to Colonel Morgan. He was a strong man, all right."

"Well, Jimmy I'm going to assign you to watch another strong man. Have you heard of General Arnold, General Benedict Arnold?"

"Yes, Sir. I was talking to him this morning at the tavern. He is a friend of Colonel Morgan."

"He is being court-martialed, Jimmy. The trial is taking place at Dickerson's Tavern. I want you to go to the trial and observe the General. I think this will expand your education. By the way, Colonel Morgan resigned his commission and returned home. I lost an excellent soldier, Jimmy."

"I know he resigned, Sir. General Arnold told me. Colonel Morgan introduced me to General Arnold one day when we were at Valley Forge. Attending the trial sounds interesting. Thank you for asking me, General."

"When the court-martial is ended I want you to come back. I'd like to hear your observations. Colonel Morgan and General Arnold are very much alike. But there are some differences. I would like to see if you noted them."

"General, I have a friend out in the hall. May I bring him in to meet you and would it be all right if he went with me to the trial? "

"Absolutely, Jimmy. Go get your friend."

Jimmy left and returned immediately with Aaron. "General, this is my friend, Private Aaron Jameson of the Pennsylvania Brigade."

General Washington looked at Aaron and said, "I remember you, Private Jameson. You helped copy the manual at Valley Forge. That was a fine job you did."

"Thank you, Sir." answered Aaron.

General Washington added, "Private Jameson, I want you to accompany Jimmy to a trial. He will explain it to you. I'll write a pass for you both to get you into the courtroom."

Jimmy and Aaron left. At the front door Jimmy asked a guard where he might find Mrs. Ford. The guard directed him and Jimmy stopped to say hello to his friend's mother. He learned that Tim was with the militia at Hobart Gap, as he suspected.

On the way to Grandma Stiles' house Jimmy told Aaron about Colonel Arnold's court martial. It turned out that Aaron knew more about the trial than Jimmy did. He explained to Jimmy that General Arnold asked to be court-martialed to clear his name officially. The General had been accused of some money problems while he was the officer in charge of the American forces in Philadelphia. Arnold denied it. But, explained Aaron, there were people in Philadelphia and in the Continental Congress who didn't like him. They said he was too arrogant and liked high-living too much. What they didn't say was that they were also very jealous of the man. Arnold's military record was above any criticism. He was definitely a hero. He proved that at Quebec, at Fort Ticonderoga, and especially at Saratoga where both he and Colonel Morgan excelled and that made other high-ranking officers look far less able than they considered themselves—hence the jealousy. This court-martial was a chance to cut the "arrogant" Arnold down to size.

Jimmy said to Aaron, "General Washington told me that General Arnold and Colonel Morgan were very similar but asked me to see if I could see any differences. What do you think he meant?"

"I'm not sure," answered Aaron "but I think he wants to see if you can see any weaknesses in Arnold. Arnold and Morgan are very much alike. But, if I had to make a choice between the two, I would take Colonel Morgan every time. I've heard from men who served with Arnold that he is an extremely brave soldier, but also a very proud man who lets his pride sometimes get in the way of good judgment. He wants to be the center of attraction and feels slighted if he isn't given credit for his accomplishments. And he had some great accomplishments."

Jimmy responded, "Aaron, I met General Arnold this morning at the tavern. It was strange. When I told him I was going to join the army when I turned sixteen he said he hoped I wouldn't be as disappointed with the army as he was. Then later, after he told me Colonel Morgan had resigned, he said he resigned once and should have stayed resigned. He sounded very bitter. What really surprised me was that he would even mention this to me--a boy sweeping the floor in a tavern and he a major general."

"That is strange." said Aaron, "Maybe we will learn why at the trial tomorrow."

Both boys were glad to reach Grandma Stiles' house after the long walk through the snow from the Ford house. When they opened the door they were greeted by a wonderful aroma.

"What are you cooking, Grandma?" asked Jimmy.

"Venison stew." answered Grandma. "Mr. Johnson shot a deer yesterday and gave some of the meat to the neighbors. Grandpa always gave deer meat to the neighbors and Uriah took over the job after Grandpa died."

"It does smell good, Grandma Stiles," said Aaron. "I've built up a big hunger walking through all that snow today."

"Me, too," echoed Jimmy.

The next morning the boys walked to Dickerson's Tavern in the Hollow behind the Presbyterian Church. A crowd had already gathered hoping to gain entrance, but guards only admitted those who had passes. When Jimmy and Aaron approached the entrance the guard started to prevent them from entering but when he saw the pass signed by General Washington he readily let them enter.

Jimmy had never been in Dickerson's Tavern. It was a competitor to Arnold's Tavern. It was smaller than Mr. Arnold's, had no large

porch in front, but instead had a smaller entrance
way. It had only two stories. The big room was
about half the size of Mr. Arnold's. There were
seats in the back of the room and that's where
Jimmy and Aaron sat. The trial had been going
on for several days and today General Arnold was
to speak in his own defense. A long table was in
the front of the room with places for the judges.
The rest of the room was set aside for witnesses
and observers. There wasn't room for too many
people and Jimmy wondered why General
Washington wanted him and Aaron to be here.
The seat next to Jimmy was vacant, but very soon
after Jimmy and Aaron had taken their seat, this
seat was taken. When Jimmy looked up at his
neighbor he recognized him. It was Lieutenant
Samuelson, the man from the Connecticut
brigade whose soldiers helped the caravan from
Hackettstown down that last hill before reaching
Morristown.

"Good morning, Lieutenant. I don't know
if you remember me. I'm Jimmy Stiles from
Morristown. I didn't get to thank you for your
help the other morning when we arrived in
Morristown. You and your soldiers were a very
welcome sight."

"Oh, yes. I remember you. I don't know how your group managed that trip to and from Hackettstown. I don't know how you managed to get down that hill of ice without losing a sledge or a sleigh. Your effort saved the day for the army. Another day or so without food and supplies many, many men would have died of starvation. Don't thank me. We thank you. What are you doing here today?"

"I'm here to observe the trial," responded Jimmy, not wanting to be a blatherskite and mention the pass from General Washington.

Lieutenant Samuelson said, "When you showed your pass to the guard I noticed the shock on his face and how readily he let you come inside. It was almost as if General Washington, himself, signed the pass. I'm here because General Arnold wanted me to be here. He signed my pass. But, I didn't get the reaction from the guard that you did."

The Lieutenant hesitated before he asked kiddingly,

"Did General Washington sign your pass?"

Jimmy's answer was truthful and given without hesitation. "Yes. Sir, he did. He asked me and my friend, Aaron, to observe the trial and report back to him what we noticed. Why did General Arnold want you to be here?"

"For the same reason, I guess. He wanted me to tell him what I thought of the trial. I've observed for several days now. Maybe we can help each other, but you must know that I am very much prejudiced in General Arnold's favor and you will have to explain that to General Washington when you report to him."

It appeared that the trial would not commence for at least half an hour so Lieutenant Samuelson began to summarize his feelings about the trial.

"I have served with General Arnold since 1775. I was only fifteen then and I volunteered to join a group that the general was organizing in Connecticut. It was to go to Massachusetts to help, just after the war began at Lexington. He was called Captain Arnold then. Anyway, I've been with him ever since. I was with him when he led the group that took Fort Ticonderoga. I was with him on the march to Quebec. I fought alongside him when he was wounded there. I was with him at Valcour Bay. I was with him at Danbury, when he chased the British out, and I was with him at Saratoga. I was there when General Gates held him back at Freeman's Farm and I was with him when, contrary to General Gates command, he attacked the British line at Bemis Heights and won the battle, and I was with him when he was wounded again. He was the hero of Saratoga, not General Gates. If it were left up to the cowardly Gates we would have lost to the British that day. General Arnold is the fightin'est man I know. The only man that comes close to him in fightin' is Daniel Morgan. Do you know him?"

Before Jimmy could respond, the lieutenant continued,

"Morgan and the General are both alike. For me, either one can whip his weight in wildcats. Just like Morgan, is the treatment the General is getting with this court-martial. Morgan wouldn't take the abuse so he quit the army and went home to Virginia. If they aren't careful Arnold is going to do the same--quit and go home to Connecticut—and then they'll lose the best general they've got. I hope you tell General Washington those exact words, Jimmy Stiles."

"I think General Washington already knows that, Lieutenant Samuelson." responded Jimmy.

Just then an officer of the court called everyone to order and the proceedings for the day began. General Arnold had the floor pleading his own defense. He wore a magnificent uniform. He walked in front of the table looking at every one of the judges including his old friend, General Henry Knox. It was General Knox who General Arnold asked at Valley Forge to witness his signature on the oath of allegiance to his country. As General Arnold walked back and forth everyone noticed his limp. That limp reminded those in attendance and those judging him of what he--more than anyone in the room-- had given in service, sacrifice and pain to his country.

Jimmy listened carefully to his words and could see the pain and humiliation this proud man was going through as he defended his honor before judges who could never be his equal. Jimmy thought that perhaps it was best if the General had resigned like Daniel Morgan did, rather than go through this torment. He remembered the General's words yesterday at Arnold's Tavern—"I resigned once. I should have stayed resigned."

General Arnold had stopped talking. He stood for several moments before the judges'

195

table, looked at each judge, turned and went to his chair. There were a few moments of silence until the officer of the court announced that there would be a recess. With that the judges all rose and left the room. There was an immediate outbreak of noise as the spectators began talking among themselves. General Arnold sat silently-- not moving a muscle.

Jimmy turned to Lieutenant Samuelson and asked, "Now what will happen, Lieutenant?"

"The judges will make their decision and return to the room to announce it. I don't know how long that will take, Jimmy. If their minds are already made up, it won't take long. If not, it could take hours or maybe they might wait until tomorrow."

A half hour passed before the court officer returned and called for order in the room. The judges took their places and gave their written decision to the officer who then read it to the spectators.

General Arnold was acquitted of all charges except two. The judges must have felt these two charges were minor for they recommended that General Arnold be given a reprimand by General Washington.

Lieutenant Samuelson explained to Jimmy, "A reprimand is like a scolding your father might give to you for doing something wrong. A scolding is a lot easier to take than a whipping and a whipping is something you might get if what you did wrong was really bad wrong. General Arnold is only getting a scolding."

"That's good," responded Jimmy.

"No, it isn't," snapped the Lieutenant. "General Arnold will not be satisfied with anything but a full acquittal and an apology for even bringing charges against him. He is a proud man, Jimmy. This isn't the first time he has been accused by others—others, who are jealous of the General's reputation. I can remember when he was charged with misusing the funds he was given to conduct the expeditions to Ticonderoga and to Quebec. The charges were false. I know for a fact that the General used his own money when the funds he was given by Massachusetts were inadequate. He paid our salaries, bought our food and supplies. He even supplied our weapons and ammunition with his own money. Misused funds! Bah! He's a hero to me and always will be. Reprimand? Bah! He should be honored by all those judges and by the Continental Congress, as well.

"Mark my word, Jimmy. The General will not take this. He'll resign before he'll take a reprimand and these fools—these jealous fools want him reprimanded. They're not worthy to shine his boots."

With that the outraged Lieutenant stormed out of Dickerson's Tavern and started walking up the hill toward the Green.

It was only four hours after noon but the January sun was already setting as Jimmy and Aaron walked home to Grandma Stiles.

The next morning the boys walked to General Washington's headquarters at the Ford house. They gained admittance and waited in the corridor for admission to see the General. In a few minutes they were invited into the office.

General Washington was standing, looking at the burning logs in the fireplace. His back was to Jimmy and Aaron but he turned when he heard them enter.

"Good morning, boys. I guess you are here to make your report on the court-martial."

"Yes, sir," responded Jimmy.

"Sit down," ordered the General. "Tell me what you think. I don't know you well enough,

Aaron, but I do know Jimmy. I respect your thoughts, Jimmy. You don't know General Arnold and you have no reason to be partial or impartial as so many of my officers do. General Arnold can be a very difficult man to deal with and he probably has made many enemies. I don't think you're one of them. You have no reason to dislike him, no reason to be jealous of his successes. What did you think of the decision?"

Jimmy told General Washington about meeting Lieutenant Samuelson and what the Lieutenant had told him about General Arnold.

General Washington spoke, "The men who served with General Arnold are very loyal to him. He has won their respect and they would follow him into battle at any time and any place. I'm not sure the lieutenant is a good judge of the General. There is too much adoration there. But I agree with him. He is the best and fightingest general I have. I don't know what I would do without him. However, with his injuries he can't lead men in battle anymore and also, by army procedures, I have to respect the decision of the court. I know the reprimand will hurt his pride."

Jimmy listened and added, "General Washington, I have only spoken to General Arnold twice. The first time was at Valley Forge when Colonel Morgan introduced me to him. The other time was the day before yesterday when I met him while I was sweeping the floor in the big room at Mr. Arnold's tavern. What I know about the general is what I have heard from others—mostly from Colonel Morgan and Lieutenant Samuelson. When I saw him at the tavern he looked very sad. He was sitting alone at a table and when I spoke to him he seemed glad to have somebody to talk to even if it was only a boy sweeping up the room. When I asked him about Colonel Morgan he told me that Colonel Morgan had resigned from the army and had gone home to Virginia. But then he added, 'I resigned once. I should have stayed resigned.' I thought that was a strange thing to say, especially to a boy sweeping the floor. Then when I saw him at the trial and talked to the lieutenant I began to understand what was troubling him. He walked--I should say limped, because the limp grabbed my attention--in front of the officers who were judging him. He walked and he spoke and he stared at each one. He was angry and I could almost say he looked at each man as if he hated him; as if he thought each man was unworthy to judge him. And, I can remember thinking that they probably were unworthy to judge him. General, I think I saw a man who was beaten down but who was thinking that he would somehow get even with his persecutors. When the decision was read, his back was to me and I couldn't see the expression on his face. He left the room then and I haven't seen him since."

General Washington then asked, "What about the lieutenant? Did he say anything?"

"Yes. He said, 'Mark my words, the general will not take this. He'll resign for sure,'" answered Jimmy.

General Washington was again staring at the fireplace. Jimmy could see he was in deep thought. After a silent minute, he turned and said, "Thank you boys. You did a good job."

With that the meeting with General Washington was over. The two left the general's office, exited the house and walked to General Greene's headquarters.

Chapter Twenty

The British Are Coming

June 1780

The winter of 1780 continued to be harsh—below freezing temperatures, snowstorms followed by more snowstorms. The soldiers of the Continental Army still suffered, but from boredom and overcrowded conditions in their tiny huts. Thank goodness they didn't have frozen hands and feet or lung fever. Spring, with its warmer winds and the appearance of bare ground and buds, still seemed far off.

General Greene had done great work in keeping the soldiers supplied with food and clothing. Jimmy and Aaron, in their own way, contributed to General Greene's success. There were now over a thousand huts on the hillsides of Jockey Hollow with smoke coming from the chimneys. There was ample firewood and the men, though crowded together (twelve men to one 14 foot by 16 foot hut), were warmer than they were when they arrived in Morristown. Though food was still not plentiful, the soldiers were not on the verge of starvation as they were several months ago. On March 17, St. Patrick's Day, there was a big celebration. Because so many of the soldiers were Irish, General Washimgton wanted to honor these soldiers.

Once a week, Jimmy went home to see his parents. They missed Jimmy but were glad that Grandma Stiles had someone to watch over her and keep her company. Aaron was becoming one of the family and Jimmy promised that when he could he would go to meet and visit with Aaron's parents in Pennsylvania.

Meanwhile, General Washington, General Greene and General Arnold were making plans for the Spring attack by the British which they knew was coming. Spies in New York told them that British General Clinton and a large portion of his army had sailed south and seized Charleston. They believed that when he returned to New York the attack would begin with Morristown as the objective.

On Kinney's Hill lookouts were posted day and night. With any sign of British activity in Elizabethtown the signal tower would be set aflame at Hobart Gap to warn Morristown that the British were coming.

The winter had been too harsh and the snow too deep for a British attack. The arrival of spring changed that. In early May Jimmy had a visitor at General Greene's headquarters on the Green. Tim Ford had come home for several days and learned that Jimmy had been asking for him. The two boys walked across the street to the Green. Tim told Jimmy he was with a group guarding Hobart Gap, the best route through the Watchung Mountains if the British decided to take Morristown. He said there had been several threats already and described them as feints. He added that his officers expected one of them would not be a feint and there would be real fighting soon. Tim was returning to the Gap the next day and Jimmy wished him good luck.

There were several false alarms as May turned into June. The soldiers at Hobart Gap, Springfield, Connecticut Farms, and Elizabethtown, who were keeping watch on the British across the Arthur Kill in Staten Island, were becoming restless and jittery. General Washington was not comfortable with the quality of troops in Elizabethtown and sent members of his own guard there to bolster up those soldiers. Among these troops, as a volunteer observer, was Tim Ford.

On the morning of June 7, shortly after midnight, English and Hessian soldiers began crossing the very narrow Arthur Kill. Their boats came ashore north of Elizabethtown to conceal their presence from the Americans for as long as possible. They moved into Elizabethtown as quietly as several thousand men could move. It was almost an hour before they were spotted by American sentries. There was a brief exchange of musket fire and the outnumbered Americans fell back through the town toward Connecticut Farms, the next town over. The British had come and there was no time for boredom now.

Cannon fire and beacon signals were heard and seen by sentries at Hobart Gap. They, in turn, lit the beacon on Tower Hill which was seen by the sentries on Kinney's Hill in Morristown and the other lookout positions. Within minutes a runner came down Kinney's Hill and shouted the alarm at General Greene's headquarters. Morristown was alerted. The militia was called and joined with soldiers from Jockey Hollow. Within the hour men were on their way to Hobart's Gap.

Several days before, Jimmy and Aaron had asked permission from General Greene to return to their units—Aaron to the Pennsylvania Brigade and Jimmy to the Morris Militia. Now with their units and friends they were off to meet the British.

By 4 AM the first unit from Morristown was on its way to Hobart Gap. Jimmy was at Colonel Hathaway's side as they marched off. Reverend Johnes had come across the Green to see them off and Jimmy asked him to tell Grandma Stiles where he had gone and not to worry.

An hour or so after sunrise they were at the outskirts of Chatham and continued on until they reached the Gap. There they rested and gathered information about what was going on. A message from Colonel Ogden, the leader of General Washington's guard, told them to hurry on to Springfield and join Ogden's troops on this side of the Rahway River that flowed through the town.

Within two hours Jimmy's group had joined Colonel Ogden. More troops were coming from Morristown. Militia were coming from Short Hills and north, from New Brunswick, the Middlebrook area and south. More and more were arriving at every hour.

Jimmy could see British soldiers on the other side of the river but there was no fighting. Occasionally a musket shot was heard but it seemed the two sides were watching and waiting. Jimmy learned the Americans had retreated from Connecticut Farms. Colonel Ogden decided to make a stand on the opposite bank of the Rahway River. There was quite a fight but the British never came across. So now they were just looking at each other.

There were some wounded soldiers-- about fifteen or twenty-- lying on the ground several hundred yards from the river bank. Jimmy suspected they were from General Washington's guard and went over to see if he knew any of them. One soldier raised his arm and waved at him. It was Tim Ford. Jimmy rushed to his side and said,

"Tim! What's the matter with you?"

"Calm down, Jimmy. I got shot this morning on the other side of the river. It's not bad. I think it was a musket ball that got me in the right leg, in the thigh. All it got was flesh, no bone. It went in one side and out the other. It hurts like fury but it's nothing serious, they tell me."

"Is there anything I can do for you?" asked Jimmy.

"I sure could use a long drink of water. There is a spring right over there."

"Do you have a canteen? I'll fill it for you."

"Yes. It's on my side, tied to my belt."

Jimmy loosened the canteen and went off to the spring to fill it. He came back and gave it to Tim who gulped the water down and handed the canteen back.

"Could I have some more, Jimmy?"

When Jimmy returned with the refilled canteen, a wagon had pulled up and some men were loading the wounded soldiers into it.

"Where are you taking these men?" asked Jimmy.

"To Morristown," answered the soldier in charge. "We can't leave them here. If the British attack again and capture them, heaven only knows what kind of treatment those Redcoats or Hessians will give them."

"Can you take this man with you? He's from Morristown."

"Sure can. We've got several wagons. Help us load him on."

Jimmy turned to Tim and told him they were putting him in the wagon and he would be in Morristown in several hours. They carried Tim gently to the wagon and laid him down in the back. Jimmy refilled the canteen, put it in Tim's hand and then found another that he filled and placed it along side of him. Tim took Jimmy's hand and thanked him and said,

"You be careful, Jimmy. Don't let them get too close to you. Them Hessians like to use their bayonets. Guess it saves their ammunition."

"I will, Tim. You behave yourself. You'll be walking again in no time. When I get back to Morristown I'll come to see you."

The wagon gave a lurch and was on its way. Jimmy returned to his unit along the river bank. The British made no further attempt to attack and late in the afternoon moved back into Elizabethtown. That night there was a violent thunderstorm that kept the British seeking shelter in Elizabethtown and the Americans trying to find shelter in their position along the river. Jimmy got out of the torrential rain by finding shelter in an empty chicken coop. Both sides spent a miserable night.

Several days passed and nothing happened. Scouts said the British were still in Elizabethtown but didn't appear to be in any hurry to continue the fight. What were they waiting for? That was the question everyone was asking. Rumor spread among the soldiers that General Greene had been appointed to command the forces in and around Springfield and Connecticut Farms. Jimmy also heard that General Arnold had been offered the command but turned it down. Supposedly he said his leg wound prevented him from doing a good job. Instead, he asked for and got command of West Point. Then news arrived that General Clinton had returned from Charleston with many ships and many soldiers. This made everyone nervous. With all those reinforcements the British would surely attack soon.

Several days passed with no noticeable change. Jimmy and his fellow militia members were still encamped by the river. General Greene had ordered the planks to be taken from the nearby bridge in case the British did try to storm across. Many of the regular Continental soldiers were on the other side of the river close to the Connecticut Farms and Elizabethtown border. General Greene had placed General Von Steuben in charge of this group. If they were pushed back to the river, General Greene did not want the English to have easy passage, using the bridge to move on to Springfield and Hobart Gap. It was there, at the river, where Jimmy waited—one day after another.

On June 22 Jimmy awoke to see hundreds of men marching by. First came a Connecticut brigade and Jimmy caught sight of Lieutenant Samuelson. Next was a regiment from Pennsylvania. Jimmy saw Aaron in this group. He ran over to him and asked where he was going. Aaron replied that they were on their way to northern New Jersey—maybe even as far as West Point. Apparently General Washington got information from spies in New York that General Clinton was leading a group of Redcoats up the Hudson by ship to attack West Point.

What about the expected attack on Connecticut Farms wondered Jimmy? Would there be enough men to stop the British here at Connecticut Farms? Jimmy got his answer that night.

About three or four in the morning musket fire in the distance woke Jimmy. Those soldiers around him were on their feet, muskets in hand, worried looks on their faces. Word had been passed to fix their bayonets and not to retreat. This line, with the river in front of them, had to be held. There was nothing behind them to stop the British from reaching Hobart Gap and then on to Morristown.

211

The sun was beginning to rise. There was a mist lying over the river. Jimmy was on the right side of the line at a part of the river that could be forded easily even with the bridge planks gone. Further up the river it was too deep to wade across and the line there was not as strong as in Jimmy's sector. They waited as the musket fire became louder and louder.

It was about ten in the morning when Jimmy saw movement across the river. The American front line was falling back. Slowly, the figures became more visible and now Jimmy could see the Redcoats and Hessians coming as well.

The retreating Americans came to the river. Some waded across. Some walked the beams left there after the planks were removed. They scurried up the bank and joined with Jimmy's group. The enemy stopped about three or four hundred yards from the river bank. They were gathering up strength or courage or both before trying to cross. Jimmy could hear his officers telling the men to be steady and not to fire until the enemy was close enough to hit. Jimmy remembered a story told him by one of the soldiers he met at Mr. Arnold's tavern. It was about that early fight up in Boston when the soldiers were told not to shoot until they could see the whites of the enemy's eyes. Jimmy wasn't sure he could wait that long.

The militia men and the regulars were arrayed in ranks. They tried to find what protection they could—trees, rocks, ground cover. Other ranks were behind. The first rank would fire, duck down, and the rank behind them would fire over their heads while they reloaded. Jimmy didn't know how many ranks were behind him and he hoped he would be told when it was safe to rise and fire again. He could hear an officer telling them to pick out an enemy, aim low, and don't fire until ordered. Across the river Jimmy could see some movement. They were moving several cannons to the front and Jimmy wondered what would hurt worse, a cannon ball or a musket ball. He finally decided it wouldn't make much difference. He could feel himself shaking and hoped he could stay in place—like the last time he stayed in place in Springfield. It seemed so long ago but it was only three years.

Suddenly he heard the roar of a cannon, and then another. He could hear shouting from across the river and then they came. The voice of his officer was heard above the shouting, "Steady, steady."

Jimmy picked out one soldier. He was a Hessian with a pointed hat and a green uniform. Jimmy's musket was aimed right at him. He was coming down the opposite river bank and into the water when the order to fire was given. The trigger was pulled; the musket roared and Jimmy quickly began the process of reloading. He looked up and saw that he had missed. He could see the Hessian coming toward him with his bayonet pointed right at him. Jimmy scrambled to his feet, bayonet at the ready. All the training-- at Valley Forge, behind the tavern, on the Green- - was about to be tested.

The Hessian thrust his bayonet-tipped musket. He must have thought he had an easy victim as he looked at the boy in front of him. There was a look of total surprise on the Hessian's face as the boy rose to meet him instead of running. Jimmy parried the Hessian thrust as he had been taught and as he had practiced so many times. The Hessian's musket and bayonet pointed skyward as Jimmy twisted his musket, wrenched upward and tore the Hessian's musket out of his hands so quickly that the Hessian stumbled, fell to his knees and stared into Jimmy face almost as if he were begging for mercy. Jimmy made no move except to point his bayonet at the Hessian's chest only a foot away.

Slowly the Hessian backed away and then ran back into the river, not stopping until he reached the safety of the opposite bank. He looked back for a moment, then ran off toward Connecticut Farms. Jimmy picked up the Hessian's musket and finished reloading his weapon. Unbeknownst to Jimmy, Colonel Hathaway had seen the whole incident from one of the back ranks.

This assault across the river was stopped, but the fighting continued. The outnumbered militia and regulars met several more assaults, each time driving the enemy back.

An hour after the attack began Jimmy heard bugles sounding and the enemy lines in front of them began a slow retreat. The British were quitting. They were going back to Elizabethtown. The Battle of Springfield was over. Another challenge had been met.

Chapter Twenty-One

The Incident at Old Tappan

Late Summer-Early Fall 1780

Jimmy returned to Morristown the next day. The militia was relieved and the regulars remained at Springfield, Connecticut Farms and Elizabethtown to make sure the English didn't try again. He went to see his mother and father running all the way out to the farm on the Vealtown Road. After he spent several days there, he returned to Morristown to take up his duties at Mr. Arnold's tavern. Grandma Stiles was fine and he was glad she hadn't worried about him. Reverend Johnes looked in on her while he was gone.

In mid August he walked to the Ford house to see how Tim was. General Washington had left the area right after the fight at Springfield and rumor had it that he was now somewhere near the New Jersey and New York border keeping an eye on any movement of the British toward West Point.

When Jimmy arrived at the Ford house Tim was sitting in a chair on the front lawn. He looked healthy enough though his leg was still bandaged. He could walk with the aid of a crutch but the two friends decided to sit and talk.

"Do you remember what I said to you before I left Springfield?" Tim asked.

"I guess you said goodbye," responded Jimmy.

"I did, but I also told you not to let any Hessian get too close to you because they like to use their bayonets."

"Yes, I remember that. Well they didn't get close and now they've gone back to New York."

"That's not the way Colonel Hathaway tells it. He told my mother and me that you knocked the musket right out of a Hessian's hands and chased him back across the river."

"That's not quite true, Tim. I didn't chase him; he skedaddled on his own."

Tim responded, "Colonel Hathaway said you could have killed him and you let him go. How come?"

"He came at me before I had time to reload my musket. You see, Colonel Hathaway told us to pick a target and not to fire until he gave the command. Well I picked a target—a big Hessian, all dressed in green wearing one of those pointy hats they wear. When Colonel Hathaway shouted 'Fire!', I fired and missed. Before I could reload he was on me. I had no other weapon except the bayonet. With the bayonet, I knocked his musket out of his hands."

"Colonel Hathaway said you could have killed him with your bayonet."

"Tim, it all happened too fast. I do remember that at the instant I looked into that Hessian's face I saw what looked like my brother, John. I froze and in that moment the Hessian high-tailed it back into the river. I'm glad. I don't think I could have stuck him."

Tim listened carefully and said, "You're lucky, Jimmy. Next time, don't miss on your first shot. I hope you never meet up with that Hessian again because I don't think he'll look at you and see his brother's face. Anyway, Colonel Hathaway says he never saw such good work with a bayonet. He said you took that musket from the Hessian like you had been doing it for years. Where did you learn how to do that?"

"At Valley Forge. A young Frenchman, Peter Duponceau, an aide to General Von Steuben, was quite good with the bayonet. He taught me that trick. If you only knew how many times he tore my musket out of my hands before I got the hang of it. The practice on the Green sharpened my skills. I think if that Hessian hadn't been so surprised that I didn't run, it would not have been so easy."

Not wanting to talk more about it, Jimmy changed the subject.

"It's quiet around here without all the soldiers and with General Washington gone. I guess your mother is glad to have the house back."

"She's very happy. It's a big house but it was very crowded with all those people living there. Now, it is so quiet I wonder if she misses all the commotion. I heard today that General Washington and the army is at Tappan, New York. Colonel Hathaway took part of the militia up there and left the other half here to keep an eye on things. As soon as my leg is better, I'm going to join the Colonel."

"Would you take me with you, Tim? I can't stay around here sweeping floors and waiting on customers."

"I have to wait until **Dr. Campfield** says I'm ready to serve. Count on it, Jimmy. I'll tell you when I can go and you can go with me."

It was now September in Morristown. Jimmy hadn't heard from Tim and was getting restless. Compared to his adventures in Springfield, work at the tavern was tedious and boring.

Toward the end of the month Tim showed up at Arnold's Tavern. He was leaving for Tappan in the morning and told Jimmy that if he still wanted to go, to meet him then at the Ford house. Jimmy couldn't wait. He ran to Grandma Stiles' house and told her he was leaving with Tim to join the army near West Point. He made sure Grandma Stiles had everything she needed and asked her to tell his mother and father where he had gone.

The next morning he met Tim and the two began their long walk to Tappan. They weren't sure how long it would take, but Jimmy thought the change of scenery was better than sweeping floors.

In the afternoon of October 1 Tim and Jimmy entered the village of Tappan. They were surprised to see the streets crowded with people.

Jimmy asked a man what was happening and the man told him there was going to be a hanging. When Jimmy asked who was to be hanged the man said, "It was a Redcoat major the soldiers caught spying. I hear he had the plans for the defenses of West Point hidden in his boots."

When Jimmy heard this he thought if General Arnold could get his hands on this spy he'd hang him himself. Just then Jimmy spied a familiar face.

"Aaron! Aaron Jameson!" he shouted.

Aaron turned, saw Jimmy and waved him over.

"I'm on guard duty here, Jimmy. I can't leave. I'm off duty after they hang this spy."

"A man over there told me the spy had the plans of the West Point defenses on him. Where did he get them? Did General Arnold know he had them?"

"Jimmy, you'll never guess who gave them to him." Without waiting for Jimmy's answer, Aaron continued, "General Arnold did."

"Are you saying the General gave the plans to the spy? Are you saying General Arnold is a traitor?"

"Yep, that's what I'm saying Jimmy. Arnold is working for the Redcoats."

"Where is General Arnold now?"

"He escaped, so I guess he is with the British in New York. From what I hear he got out in the nick of time. As General Washington was coming in the front door at West Point, Arnold was going out the back door."

"Who's the spy, Aaron?"

"His name is Major John Andre. General Greene was in charge of the court martial that found him guilty of spying and sentenced him to hang. I was on guard duty at the court-martial and some of the officers who judged Andre were the same ones who judged Arnold back in Morristown.

"They're going to hang him very soon and I'll just bet there is not a man on guard here that wants to see him die. He's a very likeable man— very honest, very brave. At the court-martial he answered every question asked of him. Didn't deny a thing. In his own defense he said he was doing his duty and was not ashamed or sorry for anything that he did. He knew he was going to be sentenced to die.

"I heard rumors that General Washington was willing to send Andre back to the British if they would send Arnold over to him but the British refused."

Jimmy answered. "Aaron, there was a hanging on the Green several years ago. The crowd that gathered was very much like the crowd gathered here. I didn't want to be part of that crowd and I don't want to be part of this one either. I'll see you when this is over. I'll be around the corner with Tim Ford. "

"I wish I could go with you, but I have to stay here. After this is over I'll meet you over there at the Dutch Church. "

Jimmy found Tim and told him what Aaron had said. He and Tim found a quiet place by the church to sit, away from the crowd, and waited until Aaron was free.

They didn't see the hanging but they knew when it was over from the sounds of the crowd. About an hour later Aaron appeared.

Jimmy said to him, "Aaron, besides General Washington and General Greene, I've met two other men I've come to have great respect for—Colonel Daniel Morgan and General Benedict Arnold. Now I have to say I've been terribly disappointed by General Arnold. When he told me at the tavern that he should have stayed retired I didn't understand what he meant. Now I do. From what I hear, Colonel Morgan has more reason to be angry about his treatment than General Arnold does. I don't think Colonel Morgan would ever be so angry that he would commit treason. He's not as vain as General Arnold."

Just then Tim interrupted and told Jimmy he was going to look for the Morris Militia headquarters and report in to Colonel Hathaway. Jimmy watched as Tim walked away and noted that Tim showed no sign of a limp. The wounded leg worked very well considering the long walk from Morristown.

After several minutes passed, Aaron said, "I heard Colonel Morgan has come out of retirement."

"You mean he returned to the army?"

"Yep."

"After today's news I have to ask, 'Whose army?'"

Aaron laughed and replied, "Our army, thank goodness. General Gates had asked him to return and Morgan refused. After Saratoga he and Gates don't get along. But, after the mess at Camden, Morgan agreed. I understand he agreed only if Gates was not the commander."

"I've been spending too much time sweeping floors at the tavern. What was the mess at Camden and where is Camden?" asked Jimmy.

Aaron was lying back on the grass chewing on a long stem of grass. "I guess you have a lot to catch up on, Jimmy. After Springfield, General Washington figured that the British would take aim at West Point to get control of the Hudson Valley. But the war seemed to leave this area and center down South. General Gates was in charge of the southern American army and was up against the British general, Cornwallis. Anyway, Cornwallis beat the tar out of Gates at the Battle of Camden in South Carolina last August. After that, I heard the Continental Congress told General Washington to find a new commander for the South. I also hear rumors that the new southern commander might be General Greene. When you sit around waiting for something to happen, rumors begin to fly like summer gnats. Some are true; most are false."

"Where is General Washington right now?" asked Jimmy.

"I think he's at West Point but I also heard that he has been to Newport, Rhode Island to talk to the commander of the French forces that have come to help us. Once again, rumor has it that the two are planning an attack on New York to finish off General Clinton. It's getting late and winter will be on us soon so I don't expect that will happen for awhile.

"By the way, I also heard that Colonel Morgan has been given the rank of brigadier general to lure him back."

"Well, he certainly deserves that when you consider all the others that have been promoted over him. We're lucky he had more character than Arnold," replied Jimmy.

Tim returned with news that he had found Colonel Hathaway and the militia by the DeWint house, not too far away. "Colonel Hathaway wants to see you, Jimmy. Maybe we'd better go see what he wants."

Aaron returned to his unit while Tim and Jimmy walked to the DeWint house. In a field nearby Colonel Hathaway and the militia had set up camp. The Colonel's headquarters was in a tent. Jimmy asked permission to enter.

"Hello, Jimmy," Colonel Hathaway said. "I thought you would show up here. It got boring at the tavern, right?"

"Yes, sir," responded Jimmy.

"Jimmy, General Greene was asking for you and told me if you were to come here I was to send you on to him. He's with General Washington and they have some questions about the time you met with General Arnold at the tavern and about the court-martial at Dickerson's Tavern. There is a wagon leaving here within the hour for West Point. Maybe you can get a ride there."

Within the hour Jimmy was sitting in the back of the wagon on his way to West Point to meet with General Greene and General Washington. As the wagon approached West Point Jimmy noticed there were many guards. The wagon was stopped several times as the guards checked them. Jimmy had a pass from Colonel Hathaway and when the guards saw that he was cleared to meet with General Greene he was quickly cleared for entrance.

General Greene was working at a table when Jimmy was escorted into the room. The general looked up and with a big smile greeted his young visitor.

"Hello, Jimmy. It's good to see you again. I heard some mighty good things about you from Colonel Hathaway. It seems you did some very good work on a Hessian down at Springfield."

"I think I was more scared of the Hessian than he was of me. I'm very glad he decided to run off," responded Jimmy.

"Jimmy, after this trouble with General Arnold, General Washington and I want to talk to you about that meeting you had with General Arnold at the tavern. You told General Washington about it, but he wants to ask you some more questions. We are trying to figure out how long he was involved in this treason. We think he might have given away more than the plans for West Point. General Washington is busy at the moment but he will be free soon. Meanwhile, if you would wait out in the hall, I'll call you as soon as he is free."

"Yes, Sir. I'll be right outside the door."

A few minutes later General Greene reappeared and asked Jimmy to follow him. He led Jimmy past two closed doors, stopped at the third and knocked.

"Come in," General Washington commanded.

General Greene entered first; Jimmy followed.

"Hello, Jimmy. Thank you for coming," said General Washington.

He motioned for them to take seats at the large table in his office.

"Jimmy, I'd like you to tell me about that conversation you had with General Arnold at the tavern. I know you have told me about it before but I'm trying to determine if General Arnold was giving away secrets before the incident with Major Andre. If he did, we are wondering what information the British might have that we don't know about. We know now he had contacts with Major Andre as far back as when he was in Philadelphia, just after Valley Forge."

Jimmy responded, "I remember how strange it seemed that he said he wished he had resigned. Besides that I can't think of anything that would show that he was a traitor then. That conversation couldn't have lasted more than several minutes. I think I was more puzzled by why he would talk like that to a boy sweeping a tavern floor. No, General Washington, there was

229

nothing that happened then that would now, make me suspect General Arnold of treason."

General Washington was silent for a moment and then said, "Thank you, Jimmy. There is one more thing I want to ask you. Do you remember when we were at Valley Forge, General Greene asked you to help copy General Von Steuben's manual?"

"Yes, Sir. I sure do. I really felt like I was helping, more than just bringing supplies to the soldiers."

"Well, Jimmy, Colonel Hamilton was very impressed with you. He said you memorized the manual in a very short time. How did you do that?"

"I don't know, Sir. I think it is because I made so many copies of that manual that I just remembered it," answered Jimmy.

General Washington had his two index fingers pushed against his lips as if he were in deep thought, then said, "When I spoke to Reverend Johnes about you and your education he told me that he gave you a book by John Locke to read and said you would come by every so often to ask him about something in the book that puzzled you. He said you recited from the book without having the book with you. How did you do that, Jimmy? How could you remember so well what you read?"

"I don't know, General. I guess I thought everybody could do that."

Again the General paused before speaking, "Jimmy, do you still remember what was written in the manual?"

"Yes, sir."

"Could you recite what is on page four for me?"

"Yes, Sir." Jimmy began speaking very rapidly, so fast that General Washington couldn't understand him.

"Slow down, Jimmy," he commanded. "I can't understand a word you're saying."

Jimmy tried but couldn't remember when he spoke slowly.

"I can't, General. When I speak slowly it goes out of my head. I don't know why. It just does. I can write it though."

"All right. Write the words that come after the word 'arms' on page five."

Jimmy began writing and then handed the paper to General Washington, who read it and then handed it to General Greene.

General Washington spoke again, "Jimmy, when you sat in on the court-martial of General Arnold and listened to his defense, you didn't write down what he said, you memorized what he said, didn't you?"

I don't know if you would call it memorizing. I just remembered what he said. When I reported to you later I told you what I remembered."

"Jimmy," General Washington said, "I read the notes of the trial and what you told me General Arnold said was exactly what was in the notes. How did you do that?"

"I don't know, Sir."

"Tell me," General Washington continued, "Do you remember everything people say?"

"No, Sir. Only what I want to remember. You told me to attend the court-martial and listen and that is what I did."

General Washington turned to General Greene and asked, "Are you thinking what I'm thinking, Nathaniel?"

General Greene nodded his head and said, "Yes."

Jimmy was wondering what all that meant when General Washington said, "Jimmy, I want you to go into the next room with General Greene. He has some things to explain to you."

General Greene ushered Jimmy through a side door into a small room and motioned for him to sit at a table. The General sat down next to him and began to speak, "Jimmy, I have to tell you a few things before I can explain what General Washington and I want you to do. Though it hasn't been announced yet, I am being assigned to command the forces in the South. I will leave in several weeks for Charlotte, North Carolina. Meanwhile, there are four thousand French troops, right now, in Newport, Rhode Island, under the command of General Rochambeau. We have about four thousand troops stationed between here and Elizabethtown and between here and Newport. That's not counting the soldiers we have in the South. As I'm sure you know, we lost an important battle this summer in South Carolina at Camden. I'm being sent south to relieve General Gates. The situation is serious. We have not had any kind of offensive since Monmouth Court House and our troops are getting restless. Congress is getting restless. The people are getting tired of the war and many want to make terms with the British. If we don't do something soon I'm afraid we will lose the support of the French."

"What do you want me to do?" asked Jimmy.

"We have to take the offensive or we are lost. We can't do anything without the help of the French and we are having great difficulty communicating with them. Our messages are being intercepted by British patrols and too many of our plans are being read by the Redcoats. You, with your unbelievable memory, could be our means of communication. You would carry no written message or plan that could be taken by the enemy. Your youth—you are only sixteen— would fool the British and they would not bother you. You could travel back and forth from here to Newport and not arouse any suspicion from them. We would tell you what message to deliver and General Rochambeau would tell you what message he had for us. I must tell you, Jimmy, there is danger in this task. You could be captured by the British. Since you would not carry any written messages or plans I don't think they would suspect your real business."

"I hope not, General. Reverend Johnes told me what happened to his wife's sister's neighbor—a man named Hale. I don't want that to happen to me."

"I don't think it will, Jimmy."

"Yes, General. I'll do it. I think that way I can help more than just sitting around here or in Morristown."

Chapter Twenty-Two

The March to Yorktown and Victory

Summer and Fall -1781

During the winter of 1780-81 there were frequent wagon trains that traveled from West Point to Morristown. Jimmy hitched a ride on one to be home for Christmas. He stayed at his parent's home for the holidays. Grandma Stiles was there. Between his mother's and his grandmother's cooking Jimmy ate well. It was a wonderful family reunion and so good to see his mother and father and his brothers. But he was restless and couldn't wait to get back to West Point.

On his return he learned that General Washington had moved his headquarters to Peekskill on the other side of the Hudson River from West Point. It was from Peekskill that Jimmy began his frequent wagon trips to Newport, Rhode Island. Each time the wagon was filled with various goods to sell in Newport and, on the return trip, goods to be sold in Peekskill, all to fool the British. And it worked. Jimmy's head was filled with messages and plans General Washington had for General Rochambeau and similar messages and plans

General   Rochambeau   had   for   General
Washington.

In Peekskill Jimmy met Colonel Alexander
Hamilton again. He had seen Colonel Hamilton
many times during the previous winter in
Morristown but the Colonel seemed preoccupied
with other things. He had fallen in love with a
young lady in Morristown. She was General
Schuyler's daughter, Betsy, who was staying the
winter at Dr. Campfield's home near the Ford
house. Colonel Hamilton and Miss Schuyler had
been married over the Christmas holidays. Now,
the Colonel was back to his army duties. General
Washington had told the Colonel about Jimmy's
remarkable memory and the Colonel quickly took
advantage of it.   By spring Jimmy had made
several trips to Newport.   In March he
accompanied General Washington and Colonel
Hamilton to Hartford to meet with General
Rochambeau. Jimmy attended the meeting as a
servant in attendance to General Washington but
his real assignment was to listen and remember
every word spoken. Jimmy learned first-hand
what was happening in the South. At first it didn't
sound good. A lot of the problem was that the
Continental Congress was running things instead
of General Washington. Congress had appointed
General Howe as commander and he lost

Savannah and all of Georgia. Then they appointed General Lincoln and he lost Charleston. Next, Congress appointed General Gates. He was the general who almost lost at Saratoga and would have if General Arnold and Daniel Morgan hadn't saved the day. Gates lost at Camden leaving the South in chaos. Finally, Congress woke up and let General Washington run the war in the South. In October he appointed General Greene to replace Gates. With Gates gone, Daniel Morgan was willing to return to the army. He was finally promoted to a brigadier general. Things began to change. News came in February of a victory at Cowpens, South Carolina. It was General Morgan who was the victor. Jimmy smiled when he heard the news.

Jimmy's trips to Newport ended in May. Plans were made for a knockout attack on the British at New York. By June the French troops moved from Newport to Providence. Then, Rochambeau moved his troops to Phillipsburg, New York to be close to the Continental Army.

General Washington and General Rochambeau carefully examined the British forces in New York. Colonel Hamilton made frequent trips toward Manhattan stopping at the bank of the Harlem River. He was studying the

British forces on the other side but could not conceive of a plan of attack that could succeed.

Meanwhile, a large French fleet under the command of Admiral DeGrasse was known to be somewhere in the Caribbean, but the two generals did not know how it could be used. On August 14 Rochambeau received a letter informing him that DeGrasse would be sailing for the Chesapeake area and would arrive sometime in late August.

The two generals met. Jimmy attended, again in the role of a servant, but making mental notes of everything. He witnessed a daring plan taking shape. It was known that a large British army under the command of General Cornwallis was located at Yorktown on the peninsula between the James and York Rivers in Virginia. General Lafayette was already in Virginia with several thousand troops and was ordered on August 15 to move to Williamsburg to prepare for a trap. If Lafayette could keep the Cornwallis army on that peninsula until the armies of Washington and Rochambeau arrived and until the French fleet could ensure the British did not escape by sea, perhaps the Americans could achieve a victory. A decisive victory, perhaps, would force the British to make peace and recognize American independence. Perhaps.

The British, of course, knew where the French and American armies were and were hoping they would dare to attack New York. Faking an attack on New York, the French and American armies began marching south leaving enough troops behind to make the British think an attack was imminent. Using the Watchung Mountains as a shield, the fast-moving French and American armies were in Whippany on August 28. Jimmy was only a few miles from home but he kept on going. He was now attached to Colonel Hamilton's New York Brigade. On September 3 he was in Trenton. On September 5 the troops had crossed the Delaware River and were in Philadelphia. By September 9 they were at the head of Chesapeake Bay—the Head of Elk—where some troops boarded ships to take them down the Bay and then up the James River to Williamsburg. Most of the other troops, Jimmy included, had to walk. By September 16 they were in Baltimore and on September 28 in Williamsburg.

General Lafayette had successfully positioned his troops to prevent Cornwallis from escaping and now almost fifteen thousand French and American troops were ready to lay siege to the British at Yorktown.

The Battle of Yorktown began as an artillery duel. The British were trapped on the peninsula between the James and York Rivers. Their back was to the York River and the French fleet. Slowly the American and French troops closed in on British and Hessian soldiers. The line between the British and Hessian troops and the American and French troops was an arc extending from the northwestern bank of the York River to the southwestern bank. There was a swamp in the middle of the arc serving as an obstacle preventing escape. A long trench—at least four feet deep and eight feet wide—was dug from the swamp to the southeastern river edge as a man-made obstacle to the escape of those entrapped. Then the American and French forces moved closer and a second trench was dug parallel to the first. At the eastern end of this second trench were two heavily defended areas protected by logs and fallen trees. Colonel Hamilton called these obstacles *abatis*. They were designed to prevent or, at least, slow down the American and French troops. These redoubts had to be taken before the second trench could be completed.

Generals Washington and Rochambeau agreed that the best and fastest way to capture these redoubts was by a head-on bayonet attack rather than using the slow process of artillery bombardment. The French were assigned the task of eliminating the redoubt to the left, the Americans to the right. A major problem was that there was almost a quarter mile separation between the two trenches. This meant the attacking troops would be without any protective cover and would have to run and then be ready to fight when they reached the enemy's protected area.

On the evening of October 14 the attack occurred. Colonel Hamilton spoke quietly to the men explaining what he wanted them to do and demonstrating how they would get over the *abatis.* As the first troops approached the redoubts they were to fall to their hands and knees. The following troops would step on their backs and jump over the pile. Jimmy was wide-eyed, afraid, wondering if he could do what Colonel Hamilton wanted him to do. He had been in combat twice before-both times at Springfield but he had always been on defense, always the defender, never the attacker. He looked across the wide and dangerously open space he had to cross and wondered if he could meet this challenge.

The troops had fixed their bayonets and were in ranks. Jimmy was beside Colonel Hamilton in the second rank. The first rank contained the troops who were to fall to their hands and knees. The Colonel gave the command and the charge across the open space began at a run. Either the enemy was asleep or they were waiting until the Americans got closer but there was no fire from their muskets. Jimmy now could see the logs and wondered if there was a Hessian on the other side with his musket aimed at him. The logs were coming up fast. An instant later he heard Colonel Hamilton shout, "Down" and down went the first rank. Colonel Hamilton stepped on a back and was atop the logs waving the men on. Jimmy made the vault and was surprised to find no musket or bayonet pointed at him. The Redcoats and Hessians put up a feeble fight but the American bayonets were too much for them. They turned on their heels and fled back toward the river. Colonel Hamilton ordered the men not to pursue them.

At the same time the French were successful in taking the redoubt to the left. The way was now open to finish the trench to the river bank. The siege continued and tightened.

For three days Jimmy and his fellow soldiers manned the trench keeping a watchful eye on the enemy lines and waiting for the siege to do its job. On the morning of October 17 the sound of a drummer came from the British lines. Jimmy could see a red-coated drummer appear at the top of the British trench. No one fired. Then a British officer appeared carrying a white flag. He began marching across the open space. An American officer came from his trench to meet him. At the mid-point the two men met. The American officer blindfolded the Redcoat and led him to the American lines.

"Now, what?" thought Jimmy.

About an hour later Colonel Hamilton called the men together to tell them the British wanted to discuss terms of surrender. He said General Washington gave General Cornwallis twenty-four hours to submit his terms.

"We are going to have to wait here to see what happens. Keep alert. This is no time to let down our guard," added the Colonel.

Jimmy heard that finally terms were accepted and on October 19 British troops marched out accompanied by a marching band. Jimmy and all the other American soldiers formed into a line. Opposite them, about one hundred feet away, the French also formed into a line. Between these two lines, led by the band, marched the surrendering British and Hessian troops—all seven thousand of them. They stacked their arms at a prescribed point and formally surrendered. The Battle of Yorktown was over and, though Jimmy didn't know it then, the war was over.

At the end of the surrender formality Colonel Hamilton called his soldiers together and told them they were soon going home.

The next day Jimmy was informed that he was to report to Colonel Hamilton's headquarters. Arriving just before noon, he was met by a young lieutenant who took him to the Colonel.

"Good morning, Jimmy. General Washington told me to bring you to him as soon as possible. Come with me. He is at the house at the end of this lane."

Jimmy followed and entered the front door of the house to find General Washington at table writing. The general looked up and said,

"Good morning, Jimmy. Colonel Hamilton told me your unit was going home today. I wanted to speak to you before you left. I've written a letter I want you to deliver to Reverend Johnes. It concerns you. Promise me, Jimmy, that you will continue your education. Pay attention to Reverend Johnes."

"Thank you, General. I'll deliver your letter and I promise I will continue my education. I don't know how, but I will.

On the way back to his unit, Colonel Hamilton handed Jimmy another letter.

"Jimmy, this is also for Reverend Johnes. Would you please take it to him?"

"Yes, sir. I would be glad to. Goodbye, Colonel Hamilton."

Chapter Twenty-Three

The Return Home

November 1781

When Jimmy turned into the lane leading to his home he saw his mother standing near the front door. She saw him about the same time and came running to meet him. Amidst a great big hug, she began to scold him.

"Jimmy Stiles, you look awful. Where have you been?"

"Thank you, Ma. You look wonderful, too. Where's Pa and the boys?"

"They're over in the woods gathering firewood. They should be here soon. Come inside and have something to eat. You look awful. Where have you been?"

"I must look awful. That's the second time you said that. I've just come back from Yorktown, Ma."

"Where's Yorktown?"

Jimmy realized then that his mother hadn't heard about the victory at Yorktown yet. "It's in Virginia, Ma. We just beat the British there and I think the war will be over soon. At least that's what Colonel Hamilton told me."

"Virginia? That's where General Washington is from. That must be a thousand miles from here. What were you doing there?"

"It's a long story, Ma. I'd better wait until Pa is here before I tell it. Yorktown is about four hundred miles from here and I walked both ways. My shoes gave out yesterday. Do any of the boys have an extra pair around? My feet are sore but I'm glad it hasn't snowed yet."

"You sit down at the table and I'll go find the shoes."

In a minute she returned with an old pair of work shoes.

"Try these on, Jimmy. If they don't fit right, there is another pair in the barn."

They fit just right.

Jimmy's mother fixed him a large bowl of potato soup, a large cup of milk and a big slice of bread with blackberry jam.

Jimmy was home.

Early the next morning Jimmy went to Morristown. It was good to see the Green again even though fall had come and the Green wasn't green. He walked across it to the Church, found Reverend Johnes and delivered the two letters.

They sat in the last pew as the Reverend read the letters. When he finished he turned to Jimmy and said,

"Jimmy, these letters are both about you. General Washington wants me to insist that you be educated beyond the school of challenges. He said you graduated from that school at Yorktown. He now wants you to prepare for entrance into the College of New Jersey. The letter from Colonel Hamilton contains an introduction to a man in Elizabethtown, a Francis Barber, who prepared him for entrance into the College of New Jersey. He didn't go there but went to King's College instead. He wants you to go to the College of New Jersey because he knows I know many people there. They both said that you were not to be concerned about money. So, Jimmy Stiles, tomorrow you and I are going to find Mr. Francis Barber in Elizabethtown and get you started on your next challenge. Now, I want you to go see your Grandma. She misses you terribly."

List of Characters

(Though *The Harder the Conflict* is fiction most of the characters did live and the events of the story did occur. The characters are listed in the order of their appearance.)

Jimmy Stiles (real): Though the story of Jimmy Stiles is fictional, he is real. He was born on his parents' farm in New Vernon, NJ on April 28, 1764. As a teenager James Stiles served in the Morris Militia under the command of General William Winds and participated in the seizure of a British fort near Elizabethtown. His commanding officer there was Colonel Benoni Hathaway. He married Phebe Aber in 1789 and they had fourteen children, eight of whom lived to adulthood. Many of his descendants still live in the Morristown area. James died in Newark in 1841.

Elijah Freeman (fictional): Elijah Freeman was the loyal member of the Morris Militia serving his commanding officer, Benoni Hathaway.

Benoni Hathaway (real): Colonel Hathaway's activities in the story are fictional but he is real. He did become the leader of the Morris Militia following the death of Colonel Jacob Ford.

Colonel Hathaway was born in 1743 in Morristown and died in 1823.

<u>Jacob Ford, Jr.</u> (real): Washington's Headquarters in Morristown was the home of Jacob Ford, Jr., his wife and his family. Colonel Ford was the leader of the Morris Militia until his death in January 1777.

<u>Captain Joseph Stiles</u> (real): Jimmy Stiles' Grandpa is real. He was born in Stratford, Connecticut in 1706 and moved to Morristown with his family in the 1720's. During the French and Indian War he was a captain in the militia. He died of pneumonia (lung fever) on December 2, 1776. Captain Joseph is buried in the Morristown Presbyterian Church Cemetery.

<u>Comfort Stiles</u> (real): Comfort (Grandma) was born in 1709 and died in 1785. She is buried next to her husband, Captain Joseph Stiles, in the Morristown Presbyterian Church Cemetery.

<u>Joseph and Phebe Stiles</u> (real): Jimmy's parents lived on a farm in New Vernon, NJ about four miles from Morristown. Jimmy's brothers—George, John and Joseph—lived there also.

<u>Reverend Timothy Johnes</u> (real): Reverend Johnes was the first pastor of the Morristown Presbyterian Church and served from 1742 until

his death in 1794. His daughter, Theodosia, married Colonel Jacob Ford, Jr.

Jacob Arnold (real): Jacob Arnold was the owner of Arnold's Tavern located adjacent to the Morristown Green. The tavern served as the headquarters for General Washington during his first stay in Morristown in 1777.

Phebe Aber and Sarah Mathias; Sam Hathaway and Caleb Fairchild (real): The names of these two girls and two boys were taken from the roster of the Presbyterian Church and are of the same age as Jimmy Stiles. Sam did die in the small pox epidemic. Jimmy and Phebe were married in 1789.

Peter Kemble (real): He was a Tory, a wealthy resident of Morristown and a very old man. His home was near Jimmy's parents' farm and was located on the Vealtown Road which today is Mount Kemble Avenue.

George Washington (real): General Washington was made commander of the Continental Army by the Continental Congress in 1775. He brought his army to Morristown for winter encampment twice—in 1777 and again in 1779-80.

Daniel Morgan (real): Daniel Morgan did come to Morristown in 1777. At the request of General

Washington he formed a special forces group here called the Rangers

<u>Alexander Hamilton</u> (real): When Alexander Hamilton came to Morristown in 1777 he was in his early twenties and was an aide to General Washington. He was involved in the detection of an English spy, though Jimmy's participation in the discovery is fictional. Hamilton married Betsy Schuyler who was visiting at the home of Dr. Campfield. That home still stands and is located on Olyphant Place in Morristown.

<u>Nathaniel Greene</u> (real): General Greene is considered by many historians to have been the best officer on General Washington's staff. General Greene was the officer who selected Jockey Hollow as the encampment site.

<u>Jonas Van Dyken</u> (fictional): Though Jonas Van Dyken is fictional, the story of the detected spy is true. Jimmy Stiles' role in the detection is fictional.

<u>Jim Iliff and Johnny Mee</u> (real): These two men were convicted of treason and hanged on the Morristown Green in the Fall of 1777.

<u>Rachel Stiles</u> (real): Rachel Stiles was Jimmy's aunt. Her son, Job, a member of the Continental Army, was wounded at the Battle of Brandywine

and suffered the trials at Valley Forge. He was sent home to collect needed supplies and to recover from his wounds and illness. After his recovery Job returned to duty and served with General Sullivan in his campaign against the Indians in northeastern Pennsylvania. At the end of the war Job elected to remain in that section of Pennsylvania.

John Martin (real): John Martin was the owner of a Delaware River ferry near Phillipsburg, NJ. The story of the crossing is fictional.

Baron Von Steuben (real): Von Steuben joined the Continental Army while it was encamped at Valley Forge. He was from Prussia and claimed to be an officer in the Prussian Army. Von Steuben was responsible for the excellent training of the army that led to the victory at the Battle of Monmouth.

Thomas Paine (real): Thomas Paine is the author of *Common Sense* and *The American Crisis* from which the title of this book was taken. He is sometimes called the *The Father of the American Revolution*. One of only six statues of Thomas Paine in the world is located at Burnham Park in Morristown.

<u>Benedict Arnold</u> (real): Benedict Arnold, known in American History as a traitor, was court-martialed in Morristown for other offenses. The trial took place at Dickerson's Tavern during December and January of 1779-80.

<u>Aaron Jameson</u> (fictional): Aaron Jameson was the young soldier from Pennsylvania who became Jimmy's friend during many of his adventures.

<u>Peter Duponceau</u> (real): Peter Duponceau was Baron Von Steuben's aide. The story of the writing of the manual is real, however, Jimmy Stiles' role in this is fictional.

<u>General Charles Lee</u> (real): General Lee was captured by the British raiding party in Basking Ridge in the Fall of 1776. The story of his role in the Battle of Monmouth is true. Fort Lee, NJ is named for him.

<u>General Clinton</u> (real): General Clinton was the British commanding general at the Battle of Monmouth.

<u>Sergeant Troxell</u> (fictional): Jimmy's ride with Sergeant Troxell to New Brunswick is fictional.

<u>Mr. Henderson</u> (fictional): Jimmy's ride across the Raritan River with Mr. Henderson is fictional.

<u>General Lafayette</u> (real): General Lafayette, a French nobleman, served as a volunteer and without pay during the American Revolution. The description of General Lafayette's role in the Battle of Monmouth is accurate. In the spring of 1780 Lafayette came to Morristown to announce to General Washington that France would send troops and a fleet to support the War for Independence. Today there are statues on the Morristown Green honoring Lafayette, George Washington and Alexander Hamilton.

<u>Lieutenant Samuelson</u> (fictional): Lieutenant Samuelson's participation in the events of this book is fictional.

<u>Tim Ford</u>: (real): Tim Ford was the son of Colonel Jacob Ford, Jr. He was wounded during the Battle of Springfield.

<u>The Hessian Soldier</u> (fictional): Hessian soldiers were from Germany and were hired to fight for the British. They were known for their ferocity. The story of the Hessian soldier in this book is fictional.

<u>Major John André</u> (real): Major John André was the British spy to whom Benedict Arnold gave the plans for the defense of West Point. André was hanged on October 2, 1780 at Tappan, NY. He

was buried where he was hanged, however, in 1821 his remains were removed to England and are now interred at Westminster Abbey in London.

<u>General Rochambeau</u> (real): General Rochambeau was the commanding general of the French forces in America.

<u>Admiral de Grasse</u> (real): Admiral de Grasse was the commander of the French fleet that trapped the British at Yorktown.

<u>Francis Barber</u> (real): Francis Barber ran a preparatory school in Elizabethtown to prepare students for entrance into Queens College (now Rutgers), Kings College (now Columbia) and the College of New Jersey (now Princeton). He prepared Alexander Hamilton for entrance into Kings College.

GLOSSARY

<u>Arnold's Tavern</u>: Arnold's Tavern was a three-story building owned by Jacob Arnold. The Tavern was used as General Washington's headquarters during his first stay in Morristown in the winter and spring of 1777. In the story it was where Jimmy was employed. The building was moved to Mount Kemble Avenue in 1886 and became All Souls Hospital in 1891. It was destroyed by fire in 1918.

<u>Arthur Kill</u>: Kill is a Dutch word (kille) meaning a water channel. The Arthur Kill is a water channel (about one hundred yards wide) that separates Staten Island from New Jersey. It is about ten miles long and connects Newark Bay on the north to Raritan Bay on the south. On the New Jersey side of the channel was Elizabethtown now called Elizabeth.

<u>Basking Ridge</u>: Basking Ridge is a village near Jimmy's parents' farm. General Charles Lee was captured at White's Tavern in Basking Ridge on December 12, 1776 by a British raiding party.

<u>Brandywine and Germantown</u>: During the early summer of 1777, anticipating a British attack on Philadelphia, General Washington took his army

from Morristown to Philadelphia to head off the British. On September 11 the Americans fought the British at Brandywine near Philadelphia. The British won and seized the city. On October 4 another battle took place at Germantown, a small village to the north and west of the city. Again the Americans were defeated. They were forced to go into a winter encampment at Valley Forge.

<u>Black River:</u> Black River is now Chester, NJ

<u>Connecticut Farms</u>: Connecticut Farms is now Union, NJ.

<u>Court-martial</u>: A court-martial is a military trial for a member of the military.

<u>Fort Ticonderoga</u>: Fort Ticonderoga was a fort of great strategic value during the early phase of the Revolution. It was located at the southern end of Lake Champlain, very near to the northern end of Lake George. Several battles occurred there during the war.

<u>German Valley</u>: German Valley is now Long Valley, NJ

<u>Hobart Gap</u>: Hobart Gap was a passage through the Watchung Mountains that would give British soldiers coming from Staten Island easy access to Morristown.

Jacob Ford's house: This colonial home is now owned by the National Park Service and called Washington's Headquarters. Behind the home is the Park Service museum.

Kinney's Hill: Kinney's Hill is about a quarter mile from the Morristown Green. It is now owned by the National Park Service and is called Fort Nonsense. From this hill lookouts could see the beacon atop Tower Hill at Hobart Gap warning of the approach of British troops.

Lexington and Concord: These two towns in Massachusetts are where the Revolutionary War began on April 19, 1775. The war was centered in Massachusetts in its earliest stage.

Morristown, New Jersey: As the story begins in the summer of 1776. Morristown is a village of approximately 200-300 people. It has two churches, several stores, two taverns, a court house and jail. The center of activity in the town and in the story is the Morristown Green. It was and still is the center of activity in Morristown.

Northampton: Northampton is now Allentown. PA.

Potts Forge: Potts Forge is now Pottstown, PA.

Quebec: Benedict Arnold and Daniel Morgan were very close friends. In the late summer of 1775 Arnold persuaded General Washington to permit him to lead an attack on the city of Quebec. Morgan was chosen by Arnold to lead a group of men in that attack. The attack failed. Arnold was severely wounded and Morgan was captured. He was later exchanged for some British officers and rejoined the Continental Army.

Saratoga: The Battle of Saratoga in New York in the fall of 1777 was perhaps the most significant battle of the war. The American victory there convinced the French government that it should support the American cause. It was the efforts of Arnold and Morgan that led to this victory.

Scabies and Chest Fever: Scabies is a disease of the skin caused by mites. It is prevalent in unsanitary areas such as Valley Forge was. It is infectious and difficult to cure. Chest fever, like lung fever, is another name for pneumonia.

Smallpox: Smallpox is a highly contagious disease caused by a virus. During the seventeenth and eighteenth centuries it is estimated that in Europe three to four hundred thousand people died of the disease each year. Because of worldwide use of vaccination the World Health

Organization proclaimed in 1979 that smallpox had been eliminated.

<u>Suckasunny</u>: Suckasunny is now Succasunna, NJ.

<u>Tory</u>: A Tory was an American who supported the British during the Revolutionary War.

<u>Von Steuben's Drill Manual</u>: This basic manual for American military training and procedure was in use until 1812. Facsimiles of the manual can be purchased from Amazon.

<u>Vealtown</u>: Vealtown is now called Bernardsville. The Vealtown Road is now called Mount Kemble Avenue

<u>Walnut Grove</u>: Walnut Grove is now Mount Freedom, NJ.

<u>Watchung Mountains</u>: The Watchung Mountains extend in a north-south line between Morristown and the Hudson River. The mountains, about three to four hundred feet above sea level, served as a barrier between the American and British armies.

<u>Waukaukaunning</u>: Waukaukaunning is now Budd Lake, NJ.

<u>West Point</u>: West Point was a fort on the Hudson River about fifty miles north of New York City. It was located at a place where the river narrows, a strategic point on the river. Whoever controlled West Point controled the Hudson Valley. For that reason the British wanted control of West Point. General Benedict Arnold was in command of the Continental forces at West Point when he committed treason by giving the plans of the fort to the British. Today, West Point is the location of the United States Military Academy.

ABOUT THE AUTHOR

Joseph H. Dempsey is a retired high school history teacher with over thirty-three years of classroom experience. He is the author of six history textbooks.

He and his wife, Audrey, reside in Morristown, NJ and have six children and seventeen grandchildren. Audrey is the great, great, great granddaughter of Jimmy Stiles.

2803959

Made in the USA